Editor
Kim Fields

Editorial Project Manager
Mara Ellen Guckian

Managing Editors
Karen J. Goldfluss, M.A.
Ina Massler Levin, M.S. Ed.

Illustrators
Blanca Apodaca
Kelly McMahon

Cover Artist
Tony Carillo

Art Manager
Kevin Barnes

Art Director
CJae Froshay

Imaging
Alfred Lau
James Edward Grace
Ricardo Martinez
Rosa C. See

Publisher
Mary D. Smith, M.S. Ed.

YEAR ROUND ACTIVITIES for Building Thinking Skills

Teacher Created Resources

Author

Ruth Foster, M. Ed.

Teacher Created Resources, Inc.
6421 Industry Way
Westminster, CA 92683
www.teachercreated.com

ISBN-1-4206-3116-0

©2005 *Teacher Created Resources, Inc.*

Made in U.S.A.

Table of Contents

Introduction

We call the act or process of knowing, including both awareness and judgment, *cognition*. Young children can't and don't know what adults know. They are developmentally unable.

When a child is born, for example, he or she is incapable of articulating words. Despite the baby's inability to converse, it is necessary and vital that we still speak to him or her. Our talking to the child is necessary for the child's language development. The child needs to hear individual sounds put together in words and connected into sentences. Meaning is gleaned as words accompany objects and actions. From trial and error attempts, a child learns what causes a reaction.

Year-Round Activities for Building Thinking Skills presents lessons and activities that develop the cognitive or thinking process. If children are to one day grow and become knowledgeable adults, they must be provided with building blocks—a background of information and skills that will enable them someday to "get" it, to know, to think. A wealth of information is presented in a way that engages children while at the same time develops cognitive or thinking skills.

A common preschool activity is to teach children to sing the alphabet. Children memorize the song despite having little concept that the alphabet consists of 26 letters, that the letters are symbols of the language we use to communicate, and that we use these same 26 letters to form all of our words. It is our teaching of the song that enriches a child and enables him or her to more easily understand how our language code (sounds, letters, grammar, usage, and meaning) fits together. A child who has heard of and is familiar with letters has a much easier time learning how to read, for example, than those who have never heard of an "a," "b," "c," or "d."

The units presented in *Year-Round Activities for Building Thinking Skills* focus on this very concept— that just as singing an alphabet song can help a child read later on, a wide variety of other ideas and facts need to be provided as building blocks for higher cognitive concepts. The more information we provide to a child, the more he or she can absorb.

Using This Book

Every lesson contains a What, Why, How, Hands-on Practice, Class Extension, and Home Page section. The What section introduces the topic and describes the lesson specifically. The Why section provides the rationale for the activity choice, as well as a list of what skills are developed or practiced.

Details and order of steps for engaging in each activity are found in the How section. When appropriate, sample questions for the teacher to ask the students are provided. A teacher may then choose to ask more questions using the same format, but with different words and answers.

The Hands-on Practice section offers ideas for activities requiring some form of physical action that can be performed in class and that reinforce the lesson covered. For example, the activity might have students color, trace, match, or sequence cards printed with the appropriate stimulus. Pages of letters, numbers, and other items are provided so that a teacher can easily make enough copies for each student.

The Class Extension section provides a supplemental activity that reinforces the lesson while extending it to a higher level. For example, instead of identifying letters from provided alphabet cards (hands-on practice), students are instructed to go on a Search and Discover Mission to find specific letters in magazines, on signs, or in newspapers.

An informational sheet for the student's parent or caregiver, the Home Page section, can be copied and sent home with the child. It describes the day's activity as well as suggesting ways a caregiver may reinforce the lesson at home in an informal and engaging manner.

4

Choosing an Activity

Activities have been divided into Language, Math, Social Skills, and General Knowledge and Facts. Some of the activities presented in the book may seem familiar to a preschool teacher. What differentiates the activities and makes them special is the emphasis on how they can be used for cognitive development.

Other activities may, at first glance, seem too difficult for a preschool book—the teaching of even and odd numbers, for example. All activities are presented at a level that preschoolers can understand. They enable a teacher to introduce his or her students to concepts they will use and need in higher grades. They provide the building blocks for higher cognitive learning.

Although the activities within each section have been listed in a rough order of difficulty (for example, letter identification before beginning and ending sounds), a teacher is not required to go through the book in the exact order that the lessons appear. There are times when a teacher may choose to engage the class in several activities at once, omit specific lessons with certain classes, or choose a particular lesson that fits well with a class unit or theme.

LESSON REINFORCEMENT

Once specific units are covered, a teacher may choose to reinforce the concepts or facts covered in the lessons several times a week. The initial lessons introducing days of the week, months of the year, and counting tasks, for example, may take up a large chunk of time as discussion and hands-on practice is needed.

Reinforcing the lessons may take only minutes and can be incorporated into a morning circle time or engaged in any time during the day. For example, it only takes a few minutes to recite the days of the week and jump up or clap one's hands on the named day of the week. The same goes for reciting the months of the year or letters of the alphabet. A teacher can instruct students to count by 5's or 10's while they are standing in line or need to be redirected. Mastery will come with practice.

CAREGIVER AND HOME SCHOOL NOTES

This book is set up in a lesson plan format, but by no means is it the exclusive property of classroom teachers. The lessons provided can be easily incorporated into family life or home schooling. The value of this book lies in how it focuses on cognitive development while introducing basic skills needed for learning. It is a valuable tool for caregivers and home school participants.

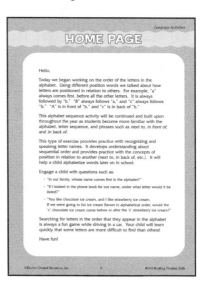

Alphabet Sequence

WHAT

Our *alphabet* has 26 letters. It is traditional that the letters are recited in a certain sequence. Filing and classification systems often use the alphabet sequence as a reference. This lesson focuses on the sequential order of the alphabet letters and how letters can be ranked as coming first, second, third, etc. Within this context, it introduces spatial concepts with proximity phrases such as *next to, in front of,* and *behind*.

WHY

Children are at an advantage when it comes to learning how to read if they are familiar with the alphabet. Awareness of alphabet letter order can provide an introduction to positional concepts, such as first, second, third, and before and after, as well. It is also fundamental for alphabetizing a list. Exercises focusing on alphabet letter sequence provide the following:

- practice and reinforcement of articulating letter names
- an introduction to the idea that in a set order there are first, second, and third positions
- an introduction to the concept that relative position determines whether a letter is before or after another
- an introduction to placing things in alphabetical order

HOW

This lesson can be taught in small increments and extended over weeks. Aspects of this lesson reinforce, and can be used in other lessons such as beginning sounds and counting.

The first step involves familiarizing children with the alphabet by singing or reciting the alphabet in order. Familiarity will come with repetition over time. A good rule of thumb is to sing the alphabet together three times a day when it is first introduced and then to reduce it to once a day as children learn the song.

As children become more proficient at singing the letters on their own, the teacher will want to incorporate a visual prompt with the letter names. A teacher may prepare and hang up an alphabet banner. As each letter is recited, the corresponding letter on the banner is pointed to. A teacher can vary this activity by handing out a laminated card of a particular letter to each student. The student holds up the letter card when that letter is recited.

During these activities, the teacher should start to point out that the sequence always remains the same. With the alphabet letter banner in sight for reference, engaging questions can be asked such as:

"Who can find the letter 's'? What letter is in front of, or before, 's'? What letter is in back of, or comes after, 's'?"

Alphabet Sequence *(cont.)*

HOW *(cont.)*

"Can you find the letters 'p' and 'a'? Is the 'p' before or after the 'a'? Is the 'a' before or after the 'p'?"

"The letters 'd,' 'e,' and 'f' are all close together. Can you find them and tell me if 'd' is in front, in back of, or in between 'f' and 'e'? Is the 'e' in front, in back of, or next to 'd'? Is 'f' in front of, in back of, or next to 'd'?"

"I'm thinking of a letter that comes after 'u.' Can you give me a letter? How about a letter that comes before 'u'?"

"I am thinking of the last letter. Can anyone tell me what the last letter of the alphabet is without looking? Is it 'a' or 'z'?"

As children begin to gain mastery over these proximity words, a teacher may want to add a number dimension. He or she can place a number banner directly underneath the letter banner, where the number "1" lines up with the letter "a," and the number "2" lines up with the letter "b," etc. The questions will focus on number placement.

"I am looking for the first letter in the alphabet. The first letter is the first one in the line. There are no other letters in front of it. What letter is first?" *(a)*

"I am looking for the fifth letter in the alphabet. The fifth letter is number five. Who can find the fifth letter?" *(e)*

"If 'e' is the fifth letter, then what letter is the sixth letter? The sixth letter is letter number six. It is . . . ." *(f)*

"I am looking for the last letter, the 26th letter. Who knows what letter number 26, the last letter, is?" *(z)*

At some point during these discussions a teacher might want to bring in a children's dictionary and have the children leaf through it. Ask them what letter follows what letter. Ask them if they think this will be true for all dictionaries. Extend this example by bringing in a children's encyclopedia. Ask what letter they think will be covered first—the "a" or the "z."

Ask the children if they notice other things that are listed in the same order as the alphabet (roll call, the phone book, books by author in the library, street names on a map legend, etc.). Discuss with children how this might make things less confusing.

Alphabet Sequence *(cont.)*

HANDS-ON PRACTICE

Make a copy of the alphabet cards and vowel cards (pages 10–27 and 90–91) for each child. Have the children place their cards in the correct alphabet sequence. A teacher can remind the students that they can sing the song or look at the banner to check letter position. As the children are physically manipulating the letters, discuss how the order never changes.

A teacher may choose to have his or her students trace, color, or decorate their alphabet cards. Some teachers may also make a smaller copy of the alphabet and have the children paste the letters onto a strip of paper (adding machine tape works well) in sequential order.

One exercise variation is to give the children only two letters at a time. Using only these two letters, have children place them in sequential order. Ask the children to describe which letter comes first and which letter comes second. Ask them if, in the real alphabet, these two letters are right next to each other or if other letters separate them.

CLASS EXTENSIONS

An exercise variation that involves gross motor skills entails alphabet letters placed on the floor in sequential order. The children can then hop, skip, tiptoe, go backward, or jump to the letter named.

The perfect scenario would be for each child to have his or her own alphabet on which to move up and down but it is a rare classroom where there is ample space. A teacher can have one large alphabet and have children take turns individually or in small groups moving between letters. Or, a teacher can use three alphabets, and divide children the into three groups.

At this point, the game can be varied. Children can return to the beginning of the alphabet, the letter "a," each time, physically feeling with their bodies each time how far "down" the letter called out is in relationship to "a." Or, a teacher may have students remain on the letter previously called out and go to the next called-out letter from there. This version allows children to physically feel where other letters are in relation to each other. A teacher may choose to call out hints such as "You are on the letter 'h.' I want you to tiptoe to 'x.' My hint is that 'x' comes after 'h' in the alphabet, and 'x' is close to the end of the alphabet." "You are on the letter 'w.' I want you to find a letter that is in front of 'w' in the alphabet. Can you find the letter 'c' in the alphabet? 'C' is at the beginning of the alphabet." "You are on the letter 'g.' I want you to jump to the letter 'o.' Try to think about what direction you will jump before you start. Does 'o' come before or after 'g' in the alphabet?"

A teacher in an advanced class might choose to give students two words, *cat* and *dog*, for example, and then have the children put them in alphabetical order. A teacher can hold up two words at a time during circle time and ask which one comes first, or he or she can place them on a board or include them on a worksheet.

HOME PAGE

Hello,

Today we began working on the order of the letters in the alphabet. Using different position words we talked about how letters are positioned in relation to others. For example, "a" always comes first, before all the other letters. It is always followed by "b." "B" always follows "a," and "c" always follows "b." "A" is in front of "b," and "c" is in back of "b."

This alphabet sequence activity will be continued and built upon throughout the year as students become more familiar with the alphabet, letter sequence, and phrases such as *next to, in front of,* and *in back of.*

This type of exercise provides practice with recognizing and speaking letter names. It develops understanding about sequential order and provides practice with the concepts of position in relation to another (next to, in back of, etc.). It will help a child alphabetize words later on in school.

Engage a child with questions such as:

- "In our family, whose name comes first in the alphabet?"

- "If I looked in the phone book for our name, under what letter would it be listed?"

- "You like chocolate ice cream, and I like strawberry ice cream. If we were going to list ice cream flavors in alphabetical order, would the 'c' chocolate ice cream come before or after the 's' strawberry ice cream?"

Searching for letters in the order that they appear in the alphabet is always a fun game while driving in a car. Your child will learn quickly that some letters are more difficult to find than others!

Have fun!

Alphabet Cards

A

B

C

D

E

F

G

H

10

Alphabet Cards *(cont.)*

I

J

K

L

M

N

O

P

Alphabet Cards *(cont.)*

Q	R
S	T
U	V
W	X

Alphabet Cards *(cont.)*

Y	Z
a	b
c	d
e	f

Alphabet Cards *(cont.)*

g

h

i

j

k

l

m

n

14   ©*Teacher Created Resources, Inc.*

Alphabet Cards *(cont.)*

k	l
m	**n**
o	**p**
q	**r**

Alphabet Cards *(cont.)*

s	t
u	v
w	x
y	z

Alphabet Cards *(cont.)*

Alphabet Cards *(cont.)*

L

M

N

P

Q

R

S

T

Alphabet Cards *(cont.)*

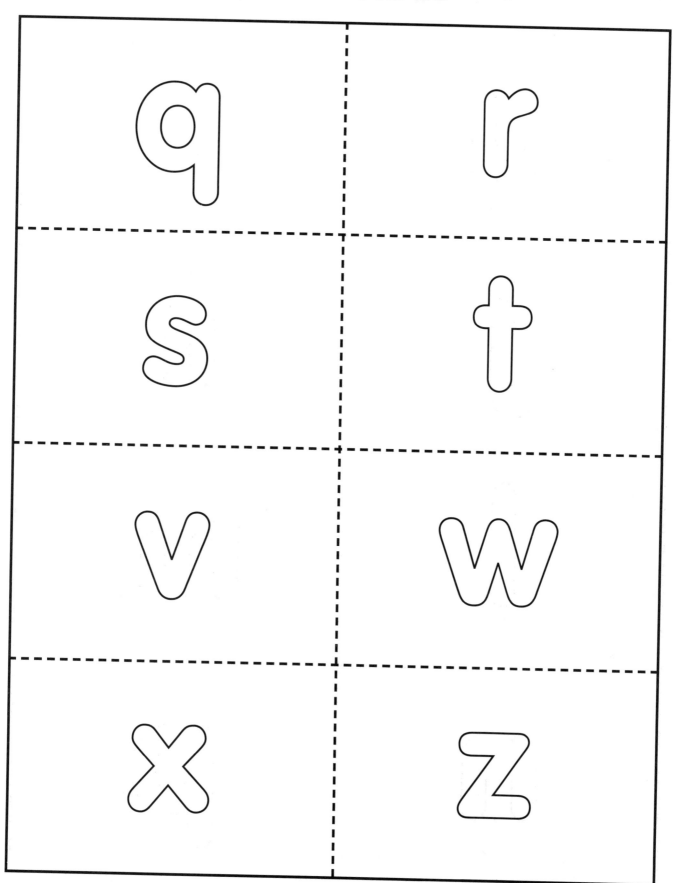

Letter Identification

WHAT

Alphabet letters are symbols of language used to communicate. There are 26 letters in the English alphabet. A child may learn to identify the symbol "A" as an "a," but his or her understanding of what an "A" is goes further. Is it still an "A" if it is white, red, or purple, or looks like this: **A a A a A a A a A a A**? This lesson focuses on the identification of letters in different sizes, colors, and fonts.

WHY

For a child to be a successful reader, he or she must learn that there are many variations of each letter. An "a" can come in all sizes, colors, and fonts.

Practice with letter identification develops the following:

- visual discrimination
- familiarity with the alphabet and written language
- association of the appropriate auditory letter name to the written letter symbol
- written language skills

HOW

First, make several cards for each letter of the alphabet, introducing different font styles. Copy the alphabet cards (pages 10–27) on different colors of paper. The teacher's set can be laminated. Next, make enough copies for each individual student.

These alphabet cards may be copied several times over the year. They can be used in many different activities.

Review the letters of the alphabet by holding up cards representing each letter. Have the children repeat the name of the letter several times. Make sure that you hold up the same letter in several different sizes and colors. Each time, ask engaging questions such as:

> "Look! This letter is now blue. Is it still an 'a'?"

> "Oh, this letter has gotten bigger! Is it now a 'b' instead of an 'a'?"

Have the children trace the letter in the air several times. Direct them to:

- Make the letter "a"
- Make the letter "a" really, really, really big! Is it still an "a"?
- Make the letter "a" really, really, really small! Is it still an "a"?

Engage the children physically and provide variety by having them trace the letters with their fingers on their hands, bottoms of their feet, on their foreheads, on each other's backs, etc.

You can settle or quiet children down by having them close their eyes and imagine that the letter is blue, red, white, black, orange, etc., or even on the side of a school bus, cereal box, chalkboard, side of a zebra, etc. Continue to ask:

> "You changed that letter from blue to red, but is it still an 'a'?"

Letter Identification *(cont.)*

HOW *(cont.)*

"You wrote the letter on the side of a lion, but is it still an 'a'?"

Engage the children on a Letter Search and Discovery Mission by holding up letters and having them find matching letters throughout the classroom. Have students focus on one letter, make their way through the alphabet sequentially, or pick letters that fit into that day's lesson plan.

"Your name begins with 'S.' Let's see if we can find five examples of words beginning with an 's.'"

"I see a blue 'a.' It is in the back of the room. Can you find it?"

"What will we find first—a big 'F' or a little 'f'?"

Note: This lesson can be a series of mini-lessons, with one or two letters being the focus of each day. Uppercase and lowercase letters may be done on the same or separate days, depending on the level of the students.

HANDS-ON PRACTICE

Children can color or decorate their alphabet cards using different colors. They can then match their cards to the same letters that another child has colored. A pairing game can also be played where children match lowercase letters to uppercase letters.

If a tactile approach or reinforcement exercise is desired, a teacher may have children create raised letters by having them glue or paste beans or other small objects inside the bubble alphabet letters and vowels (pages 23–27 and 90–91).

In addition, there are Letter Identification Practice pages (pages 31–43). Copies can be made for each child. Children match the stimulus letter printed on the left to the one in the row of letters on the right. Note that there is a matching uppercase and lowercase letter in each row of letters. Teachers can have children match the stimulus letter to both the uppercase and lowercase letter, or they can choose to have children match only the uppercase or lowercase letter. A teacher can make two copies of each exercise sheet, if  desired, so that children match the uppercase letter on one page and the lowercase letter on the other if they feel it is too confusing for children to match both on the same page.

CLASS EXTENSION

Don't forget about magazines and newspapers! Send children on a Search and Discover Mission to find:

- five examples of an "o" on one newspaper page
- a big "H" and a little "h"
- the same letter, but in two different colors
- the entire alphabet
- the letters in their names, the name of the month, a vocabulary word, or words they like to say

HOME PAGE

Hello,

Today we worked on letter identification. A letter is the same even if it is printed in different colors, sizes, or fonts (styles).

Practice with letter identification helps a child associate the proper spoken name of the letter to the written one. This familiarity will help a child recognize the same letters printed in different places and books that are different colors, sizes, or fonts.

Entertain your child by going on a Discovery Mission. Even though your child may be a passive passenger in a car, or waiting in a store line, or sitting in an office, he or she can still engage in a letter search. By looking at road and store signs or the print on posters and boxes, your child can seek out and find letters. Go through the alphabet in sequence or look for specific letters. For example,

"I see a green 'A.' It is on a white sign, and it is on the left side of the car—the same as I. Can you find it?"

"See that truck in front of us? Is that an 'm' or an 'n' written on it? Those letters look so much alike!"

"Can anyone tell me a letter off a license plate?"

"Look! There's (name of restaurant). Does that restaurant have an 'm' in its name?"

Have fun!

Name _____

Letter Identification Practice *(cont.)*

Draw a circle around the matching uppercase and/or lowercase letter.

Q	g q G Q
R	r B R s
S	m s S w
T	T I f t

Name _____

Letter Identification Practice *(cont.)*

Draw a circle around the matching uppercase and/or lowercase letter.

U	n	U	O	u
V	u	X	v	V
W	w	M	W	m
X	v	x	X	M

Name _____

Letter Identification Practice *(cont.)*

Draw a circle around the matching uppercase and/or lowercase letter.

Y	g Y R y
Z	m z Z l
a	e a A t
b	B d b g

Name _____

Letter Identification Practice *(cont.)*

Draw a circle around the matching lowercase and/or uppercase letter.

c	t C e c
d	h d s D
e	r g E e
f	f t t F

38

Name _____

Letter Identification Practice (cont.)

Draw a circle around the matching lowercase and/or uppercase letter.

w	m	n	w	W
x	m	x	f	X
y	Y	v	y	m
z	z	w	Z	x

Beginning Sounds

WHAT

Children are taught to associate alphabet letters with sounds. This is a developmental step necessary for reading. This lesson focuses on developing the tie between phonetic letter sounds and words that begin with the corresponding letters.

WHY

To be good readers, children need to become familiar with letters and their corresponding sounds. Tying beginning word sounds to letters helps a child:

- strengthen the association between letter and sound
- develop skills for sounding out words
- sort words by beginning letters
- build vocabulary
- practice alphabet letters
- reinforce the alphabet sequence

HOW

Several games are presented that allow children to practice finding words that start with different letters and sounds. A teacher may present these games in any order that he or she desires. A teacher may choose to play these games several times over the year.

Game One: Choose a letter and a letter sound. This may be done in various ways. A teacher may:

- go through the alphabet in sequence
- go through the class, each day choosing a letter with which a child's name starts
- choose the same letter that is the beginning letter for the name of the day, month, season, school, etc.

Repeat the word, letter, and sound several times. For example, if the day is Monday, a teacher might say, "Monday, Monday, Monday, mmmmmm, mmmmmm, mmmmmmm, 'm,' 'm,' Monday, 'm,' I want the 'm' sound. I want mmmmmmm. Let's see, can I find more words that begin with the mmmmmmmm sound?"

Have each child come up with a word. These words might be other children's names that start with the same letter, nouns, or verbs. For example, *Meredith, Marie, Marcus, man, mouse, mile, music, Mrs., mask, making, mixing,* etc. Children may be led to an answer the first time a letter is used, but over time, they will begin to recall words from previous times the game was played.

Game Two: Using the alphabet letter order, take turns coming up with words that match the letter. Children especially love to do this with animals, and a list of animals has been provided (page 47). Of course, there are many more animals than those listed, but it may help you through some tough ones— like the "x," "y," and "z"!

A game might proceed as follows: the first child says *anteater;* the second, *bear;* the third, *cat;* the fourth, *dog;* and so on.

Beginning Sounds *(cont.)*

HOW *(cont.)*

This game can be varied by having children say any word that comes to mind (*ape, brain, cold, dig, everything,* etc.), different types of food (*apple, berry, cream, doughnut, egg, fish,* etc.), different names (*Adrianne, Bak, Corey, Dai, Endo, Fred,* etc.), or different places (*Alaska, Bakersfield, Canada, Delaware, England,* etc.).

Game Three: This game can be presented as a Detective game. Children must find objects in the room or in the environment around them that begin with a certain letter. This can be done by naming a letter or by going through the alphabet. If the letter "r" is named, for example, make the "r" sound several times and then look for corresponding objects. Children might find a picture of a rooster, a "real" person, a "resting" child, a road, etc. Or, they can find red items such as a red book, a red hat, a red ball, a red shirt, etc.

If children are to seek objects in alphabetical order, they will quickly find that some letters are much more difficult to work with than others! A series might start with *asphalt, boy, car, ditch, earth,* etc.

A teacher may choose to point to the corresponding letters of the alphabet or hold up cards so there is visual reinforcement if this game is played at a circle time. The game is not limited to circle time; it can be played anytime and anywhere throughout the year for reinforcement.

HANDS-ON PRACTICE

Make copies of the Animal Alphabet Cards (pages 48–52) for each child. Children can color the cards and trace the letters. Have children match letters of the alphabet to the pictures of objects that begin with those words. If desired, the pictures can be pasted next to each other on a sheet of paper.

If the game chosen is one that involves animal names, have children act like the animals named. For example, a child can slither on the floor like a snake, wave his or her arm as if it were a trunk for an elephant, and laugh like a hyena.

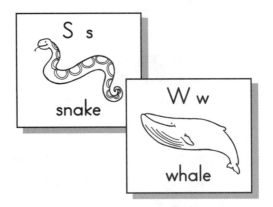

CLASS EXTENSIONS

Look up animals with which children are unfamiliar in an encyclopedia or in a book so that they can see a picture of them.

Take a child's dictionary and show how words are listed in order of beginning letter. Read some of the words aloud. Have the children repeat the words after you say them, each time stressing the beginning sound. Children will enjoy this same activity with a dictionary of names.

HOME PAGE

Hello,

Today we worked on the beginning sounds of words. We did this by listing words that began with the same sound (for example, *bat, boy, butterfly, bike*). We also went through the alphabet, finding words that began with each letter (for example, *apple, bee, carrot, dessert, eat, fork,* and so on).

These activities focus on some of the skills needed for reading later on. They also reinforce the alphabet, letter/sound connections, and build vocabulary.

Entertain your child by playing some of the games we did.

Game One: Pick a letter and find some more words that start with that letter. For example, the letter "s": *snake, swallow, sit, seat, silly, sandwich.*

Game Two: Go through the alphabet and list, in alphabetical order, every animal that you know. For example, *ant, bee, cat, dog, emu, fox, gecko,* etc.

Some unfamiliar animal names:

quelea (bird)	quahog (clam)	quail
umbrella bird	uakari (monkey)	urchin
vampire bat	vole	whooping crane
xenopus (frog)	Xantus hummingbird	velvet ant
yucca moth	yellowhammer (bird)	yak
zebra swallowtail butterfly	zorille (weasel)	

This game can be repeated with any word, names, places, or foods. Some animal names have been listed above to help you through some of the more difficult letters.

Game Three: Have your child find objects that start with the letters of the alphabet. This is a great activity when children are passengers in a car or waiting somewhere. For example, *asphalt, boy, car, dog, earth, face,* etc.

Have fun!

Animal Names for Use in Alphabet Games

aardvark	indri (lemur)	rat
anaconda	jackal	rhinoceros
anteater	jaguar	salamander
baboon	jaguarundi	seal
bear	kangaroo	snake
bison	kangaroo rat	tapir
camel	koala	tiger
cat	lemur	turtle
cougar	lightning bug	uakari (monkey)
deer	llama	umbrella bird
dog	monkey	urchin
duck	mouse	vampire bat
eel	mule	velvet ant
eland (African antelope)	nematode (worm)	vole
elephant	newt	wallaby
ferret	nightingale	walrus
fox	opossum	whale
fox terrier	orca (whale)	whooping crane
giraffe	otter	Xantus hummingbird
gnu	pig	xenopus (frog)
gorilla	porcupine	yak
hare	prairie dog	yellowhammer (bird)
horse	quahog (clam)	yucca moth
hyena	quail	zebra
iguana	quelea (bird)	zebra swallowtail butterfly
indigo snake	raccoon	zorille (weasel)

Animal Alphabet Cards

A a

ant

B b

bear

C c

cat

D d

deer

E e

elephant

F f

fox

Animal Alphabet Cards *(cont.)*

G g
giraffe

H h
horse

I i
iguana

J j
jaguar

K k
kangaroo

L l
lion

Animal Alphabet Cards *(cont.)*

M m
monkey

N n
newt

O o
otter

P p
porcupine

Q q
quail

R r
raccoon

Animal Alphabet Cards *(cont.)*

S s
snake

T t
tiger

U u
urchin

V v
vole

W w
whale

X x
xenopus

Animal Alphabet Cards *(cont.)*

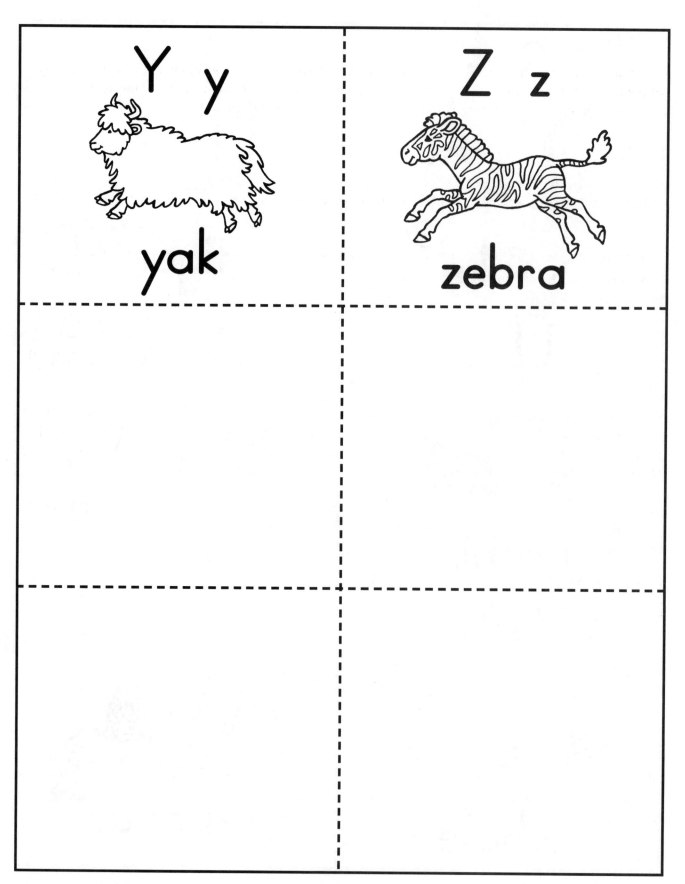

Ending Sounds

WHAT

Children are taught to associate alphabet letters with sounds. This is a developmental step necessary for reading. This lesson focuses on strengthening the tie between phonetic letter sounds and the corresponding letters by working with the ending letters and sounds of words.

WHY

As children become mature readers, they advance from paying attention to what letter a word starts with to what letter the word ends with. Listening for and learning word-ending sounds enables a child to:

- strengthen the association between letter and sound
- develop skills for sounding out words
- build vocabulary

HOW

Several games are presented that allow children to practice finding words that start with the last letter of the word presented before.

When these games are first introduced, children may have a difficult time hearing the last letter. They might need to be led to the answer. Exaggerating the last sound of the word is one way to do this. For example, if the word spoken is *cat*, instead of emphasizing the first letter and sound, the teacher stresses the last. "Cat, cat, 't.' Do you hear the 't' sound? What letter makes the 't' sound?"

The first time a game is played, a teacher may also decide to hold up a word and have children point to the beginning of the word and the end of the word. This reinforces what part of the word is being emphasized.

Game One: Say a word that has an easy-to-pick-out sound at the end of the word, such as *cat*. Have children come up with words that end with the same sound. Often, this activity can develop or reinforce rhyming skills. For the word *cat*, for example, words that end in the same sound can be *bat*, *rat*, *sat*, *pat*, and *fat*. Other words might be *fast*, *past*, *mast*, *cast*, and *biggest, smallest, tiniest*, etc.

Game Two: This is a variation of Game One. In this case, do not limit the words chosen to one category. Any word can be chosen as long as the ending sound of the first word is the beginning sound of the second word. A possible series might be: *hello—otter—rat—trick—king—guppy*.

There will be many times when the last letter of a word is not heard, as in the cases of *time, dime,* and *lime*. Simply explain that for many words, one does not say the last letter sound. Do not make the children search for the last letter. Promptly give them the answer, and encourage them to continue with the game. This response will make children more familiar with words where the last letters are silent when they begin to read. Depending on the situation, a teacher may decide to say, "Even though the last letter is one we cannot hear, the last sound we can hear is _____, and so that is the letter sound we will use."

Ending Sounds *(cont.)*

HOW *(cont.)*

Game Three: Say the name of any animal. Take the last letter of the animal name. Make that letter the first letter of the next animal. For example, if the word *cat* is said, the next animal chosen needs to start with a "t." If the word *tiger* is chosen, the next word needs to start with an "r." A possible series of words might be *elephant—tick—kangaroo—otter—rhinoceros—snake* and so on. Please note that a list of animal names is provided in the Beginning Sounds lesson (page 47).

Game Four: This is a variation of Game Three. Instead of saying an animal, say a word that has a geographic connection. It could be the name of a city, street, town, ocean, river, mountain, or country. For example, if one starts with *California*, the next place must start with an "A." One might choose *Australia*. A possible series might be: *Texas—San Diego—Oregon—North America—Antarctica—Asia,* etc. You will quickly discover that there is a large call for places that start with an "A!"

A teacher may choose to play these games several times over the year.

HANDS-ON PRACTICE

Have children take a section of a newspaper (one comic, perhaps, or a headline). A teacher may choose to copy this section so that everyone has the same exercise. Have children circle or underline the last letter of every word. A teacher may also choose to copy one or two pages of a beginning reading book for this exercise.

CLASS EXTENSIONS

When Game Three is played, a class might look up animals about which children are unfamiliar in an encyclopedia or other book so that they can see pictures of them.

When Game Four is played, be sure to display a map. Point to the places named. Children cannot read yet, but they still might be able to pick out a country that starts with a particular letter by identifying the beginning letter. This exercise familiarizes children with a map and how different places are located across it.

54

HOME PAGE

Hello,

Today we worked on ending word sounds. We did this by listing words that end with the same sound (for example, *bat, cat, rat, sat, elephant, foot, feet, boot*). Some of the words we listed were great for rhyming practice!

We also found words that started with the letter with which the previously spoken word ended. The word *bat* ends with "t," so our next word started with a "t." A possible word series would be: *dog—gopher—rhino—otter—rat—tiger,* and so on.

These activities focus on some of the skills needed for reading later on. They reinforce the alphabet and letter/sound connections, and help a child become aware of ending word letters and how they sound. Entertain your child by playing the same animal game we did. Here are some unfamiliar animal names that may come in handy.

quelea (bird)	quahog (clam)
quail	umbrella bird
uakari (monkey)	urchin
vampire bat	viscacha (S.A. rodent)
velvet ant	xenopus (frog)
Xantus hummingbird	yak
yellowhammer (bird)	yucca moth
zorille (weasel)	zebra swallowtail butterfly

Alternative: Geographical locations, as well as any word or topic (names, foods, etc.), can be used instead of animal names for variation.

For example, *California—Alabama—Antarctica—Austin— New Jersey—Yorktown,* etc.

Have fun!

Plurals

WHAT

A *plural* is the form of a word which shows that more than one is meant. Most plurals are formed by adding the letter "s" or "es," as *cat* to *cats* and *box* to *boxes*. Some plurals are formed in different ways (*man* to *men*) and others remain the same (*sheep* to *sheep*). This activity focuses on how words and their plurals are pronounced.

WHY

When a child adds a word to his or her vocabulary, that word's plural is not added automatically. Ability with plurals shows that a child understands the difference between singular and plural, or one and more than one. Some children learn to add the "s" sound over time by listening to the speech around them. Other children need more direction. Activities with word plurals:

- increase a child's vocabulary
- reinforce the concept of singular and of plural
- provide practice with word pronunciation

HOW

A teacher may choose to laminate a large letter "s" to use as a visual prompt for this activity. He or she may also choose to provide a smaller "s" for each child to hold up when the plural of a word is spoken. (See page 58 for samples.) The small s's can be laminated and attached to craft sticks for student use.

First, start a discussion by making a loud and long sssssssssssssssss sound. Ask children if they have ever heard it before. Many children will think it sounds like a snake. Tell them they are correct, but it is also something else. Redirect them by saying several words aloud, emphasizing the "s" at the end. For example, *bats, snakes, books, elephants, shirts, eyes, hands,* etc.

Once children have come up with the idea that the "s" sound is often at the end of words, ask them if they know the difference between *bat* and *bats*, *snake* and *snakes*, *book* and *books*, *elephant* and *elephants*, *shirt* and *shirts*, *eye* and *eyes*, and *hand* and *hands*. Some children will realize that the difference is more than one. Reinforce this concept by saying, "Yes, we put an 's' on the end of words when we mean more than one."

At this point, a teacher may want to recite a list of words and have the children respond with the plural of each word. If the children have "s" cards, they may hold up the "s" every time they speak the plural.

A sample list might include the following words:

finger	teacher	truck	nose	cake
thumb	turtle	garbage truck	ankle	pencil
leg	dog	alligator	cheek	pen
boy	cat	crocodile	dinosaur	crayon
girl	car	lion	bird	eraser

Plurals *(cont.)*

HOW *(cont.)*

Now, the teacher should introduce the words whose plurals are not made by adding an "s." He or she might want to lead the discussion by saying, "You are too good at this! This is too easy for you! You know how to make more than one with most of the words in the world! Now it is time to learn the ones that are not so simple."

Recite each word on the list below and ask the children to try to think of the plural of that word. Have them repeat the plural several times. Some teachers may want to go through the list completely and then say, "Let's say those words again. I am going to see how many you remember."

foot ——— feet	tooth ——— teeth
child ——— children	mouse ——— mice
man ——— men	woman ——— women
person ——— people	goose ——— geese

At this point, a teacher may want to call out a combination of words whose plurals are made by adding an "s" and those that change like the ones in the list above.

Next, a teacher should explain that there is one more type of plural. Recite these words and ask the children what word they would use to mean more than one.

deer ——— deer	sheep ——— sheep
fish ——— fish	pants ——— pants

Once the children have repeated these words several times, a teacher should ask the children how someone could tell if the words mean one or more than one.

The response should be something like, "By listening carefully, you can figure out whether the speaker means just one, or more than one." Next, the teacher should say these sentences, each time having the children consider whether there could be just one or more than one.

"I saw a deer."
"I saw lots of deer."
"The farmer has a sheep."
"The farmer has lots of sheep."
"I caught a fish."
"There are fish in the ocean."
"I am wearing pants."
"There are ten pairs of pants in this classroom right now."

As a final exercise, a teacher can say a word and have the children repeat the plural. He or she can combine words from all three lists.

A variation of this exercise is to take turns with each child saying a word and having the class respond with that word's plural.

Plurals *(cont.)*

HANDS-ON PRACTICE

Make copies of the Plurals practice sheets (pages 60–64). On the Plurals Practice sheet (page 60), children first trace the letter "s" on the bottom of the page. Next, they can cut out the letter blocks and paste the letter on the side of the paper that has the plural number of objects. On Plurals Practice (page 61), children draw a line from each stimulus word to its corresponding picture. On Plurals Practice (pages 62–64). Children circle the appropriate pictures to match the words. Even if they cannot read, they can use the "s" at the end of the word to determine whether they draw the line or circle the single object or the multiple objects.

CLASS EXTENSION

Have children stand alone or in small groups around the classroom. Appoint one child to point to each individual and group and say, "person" or "people," and "child" or "children." Have children take turns naming the groups. Have children alter group sizes each time.

S	S	S	S	S
	S	S	S	S
	S	S	S	S
	S	S	S	S
	S	S	S	S

HOME PAGE

Hello,

Today we talked about words and their plurals. We talked about plurals that are made by adding an "s" (*bat, bats; chair, chairs; table, tables*). We also brought up plurals that change (*person, people; man, men; child, children*) and those that don't (*sheep, sheep; deer, deer*).

This activity increases a child's vocabulary. It provides practice with word pronunciation. It reinforces the concept of singular (one) and plural (more than one).

Entertain your child by asking questions about plurals. This may be done in a couple of ways:

- you say a word and your child comes up with the plural

- your child says a word, and you come up with the plural

- you say a plural word, and your child has to come up with the singular and use it in a sentence. (For example: We are all wearing pants in this car. *I have on a pair of pants.*)

Have fun!

Name _____

Plurals Practice

Paste your "s" on the side that has more than one.

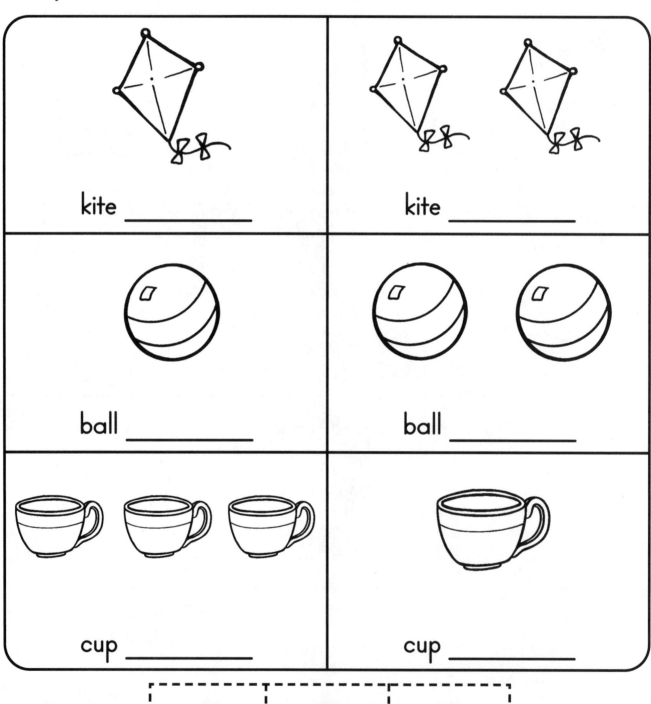

kite _____   kite _____

ball _____   ball _____

cup _____   cup _____

S   S   S

60

Name _____

Plurals Practice *(cont.)*

Draw a line to match each word to the correct side.

Name _____

Plurals Practice *(cont.)*

Circle the correct picture to match each word.

Name _____

Plurals Practice *(cont.)*

Circle the correct picture to match each word.

Name _____

Plurals Practice *(cont.)*

Circle the correct picture to match each word.

 **apple**

 **dolls**

 **bananas**

 **car**

Rhyming

WHAT

A *rhyming* word is one that has the same ending sound as another. For example, the word *cat* rhymes with the words *bat, sat, mat,* and *pat.* This activity provides practice identifying and articulating words that rhyme.

WHY

Rhyming activities are used in beginning reading lessons. Rhyming practice can engage children while they are doing the following:

- developing listening skills (beginning sounds as well as the rhyming end sounds)
- providing practice articulating letter and word sounds
- developing groundwork for phonics instruction (how speech sounds are represented in writing)

HOW

Recite a series of words to the children and ask if they notice something about the words. Use these words as examples:

> *bat, cat, sat, rat, pat, fat*
> *rake, bake, cake, lake, take, stake*
> *sing, ring, bring, king, thing*
> *pet, met, net, bet, let, jet, set*
> *three, me, be, tree, see*

One may want to direct what children notice by asking them if the beginning sounds of the words are the same. Then ask them if the word endings sound the same.

Explain to the children that when the ending sounds of words are the same, we call it *rhyming.* Rhyming words have the same ending sound.

Engage the children by playing games in which the children are to play the part of Rhyme Detectives.

Game One: Start by reciting a list of rhyming words and ask children to come up with another rhyming word. As Word Detectives, the children need to find the lost rhyming words. Often, when this exercise is first introduced, or the rhyming sets being used are new, children will need guidance. To help, make the beginning sound for them. For example,

> *met, bet, p . . . ,*

Continue with the next child or group by saying:

> *met, bet, pet, s . . .*
> *met, bet, pet, set, w . . .*

Repeating each sequence with the new word will provide immediate and constant reinforcement. Do this with several rhyming sets.

Rhyming *(cont.)*

HOW *(cont.)*

Game Two: Inform the children that as Word Detectives, they are to find the word that does not belong. It is in the wrong place. It doesn't rhyme with the other words. Then, list three words, two of which rhyme. When this game is first introduced, make sure that the non-rhyming word is easy to pick out. For example,

> *park, lark, chicken*
>
> *sit, bit, alligator*
>
> *elevator, up, pup*
>
> *well, tell, dinosaur*

Increase the difficulty by putting the non-rhyming words in the middle of the list, as well as making them sound more alike (with beginning sounds and vowel sounds). For example,

> *house, smile, mouse*
>
> *pig, bell, wig*
>
> *big, bell, jig*
>
> *cook, king, book*

If children have difficulty with this, simply repeat the words for them in an easier order—with the rhyming words immediately after each other.

Once children begin to understand what a rhyming word is, a teacher may choose to reinforce the concept throughout the year. He or she can do this by practicing the rhyming games or by having a daily rhyming challenge. For this, a teacher may choose to say, "The rhyming question for the day is Do _____ and _____ rhyme?"

HANDS-ON PRACTICE

Make copies of the rhyming cards (pages 74–77). Have the children color the cards. Have them match the rhyming words with each other.

CLASS EXTENSION

Read or recite nursery rhymes and poems together aloud. After reading each rhyme, go through and find the rhyming words. Repeat them aloud. When a teacher first engages the children in this activity, and when the rhymes are still new, a teacher may want to stress with his or her voice which words rhyme. Copies of the nursery rhymes (pages 68–73) can be made for each child and formed into a mini-book.

HOME PAGE

Hello,

Today we talked about words that *rhyme*. Words that rhyme have the same ending sound. Familiar rhyming words are *cat, bat, sat, pat,* and *rat,* and *cook, book, hook, look,* and *took.*

Practice with rhyming words prepares children for beginning reading lessons. It develops listening skills as well as providing practice articulating letter and word sounds.

A fun activity for your child is to ask him or her questions about rhyming. This will entertain your child while he or she is a passenger in a car or waiting in line.

Try the following questions:

"*Light* and *tight,* do they rhyme?"
"*Light, tight,* and *fight,* do they rhyme?"
"*My* and *by,* do they rhyme?"
"*My, by,* and *cry,* do they rhyme?"

Have children find the next rhyming word:

fell, tell, *(well, sell)*
boy, joy, *(toy)*
noon, loon, *(spoon, balloon, baboon)*
lake, make, *(cake, bake, sake, fake)*

Have fun!

Humpty Dumpty

Humpty Dumpty sat on a wall,

Humpty Dumpty had a great fall.

All the king's horses and all the king's men,

Couldn't put Humpty together again.

Little Miss Muffet

Little Miss Muffet

Sat on a tuffet,

Eating her curds and whey;

Along came a spider

Who sat down beside her

And frightened Miss Muffet away.

Mary, Mary, Quite Contrary

Mary, Mary,

Quite contrary,

How does your garden grow?

With silver bells

And cockle shells

And pretty maids

All in a row.

- -

Little Bo Peep

Little Bo Peep

Has lost her sheep,

And doesn't know where to find them;

Leave them alone, and they'll come home,

Wagging their tails behind them.

Jack and Jill

Jack and Jill

Ran up a hill,

To fetch a pail of water;

Jack fell down,

And broke his crown,

And Jill came tumbling after.

One, Two, Buckle My Shoe

One, two, buckle my shoe.

Three, four, shut the door.

Five, six, pick up sticks.

Seven, eight, lay them straight.

Nine, ten, do it again.

Little Jack Horner

Little Jack Horner

Sat in the corner,

Eating a Christmas pie;

He put in his thumb, and pulled out a plum,

And said, "What a good boy am I!"

Little Boy Blue

Little Boy Blue, come blow your horn,

The sheep's in the meadow, the cow's in the corn;

But where is the boy who looks after the sheep?

He's under the haystack fast asleep!

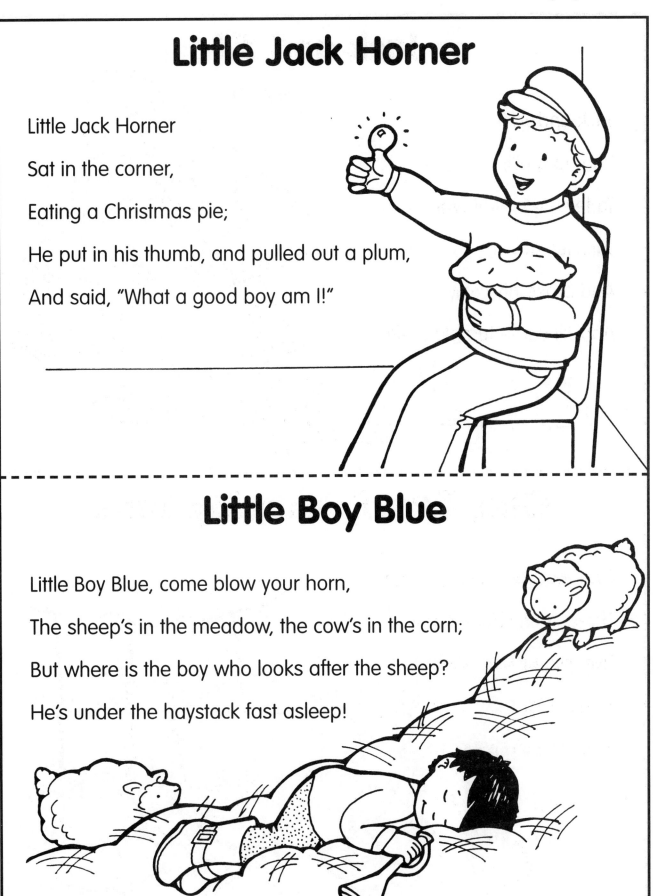

Hey Diddle, Diddle

Hey diddle, diddle

The cat and the fiddle,

The cow jumped over the moon.

The little dog laughed to see such sport,

And the dish ran away with the spoon.

Baa, Baa, Black Sheep

Baa, baa, black sheep,

Have you any wool?

Yes, sir, yes, sir,

Three bags full;

One for my master,

One for my dame,

And one for the little boy

Who lives down the lane.

Hickory, Dickory, Dock

Hickory, dickory, dock!

The mouse ran up the clock;

The clock struck one,

The mouse ran down,

Hickory, dickory, dock!

Twinkle, Twinkle, Little Star

Twinkle, twinkle, little star,

How I wonder what you are.

Up above the world so high,

Like a diamond in the sky.

Twinkle, twinkle, little star,

How I wonder what you are.

Rhyming Practice Cards

bee

tree

cat

hat

cake

rake

book

hook

Rhyming Practice Cards *(cont.)*

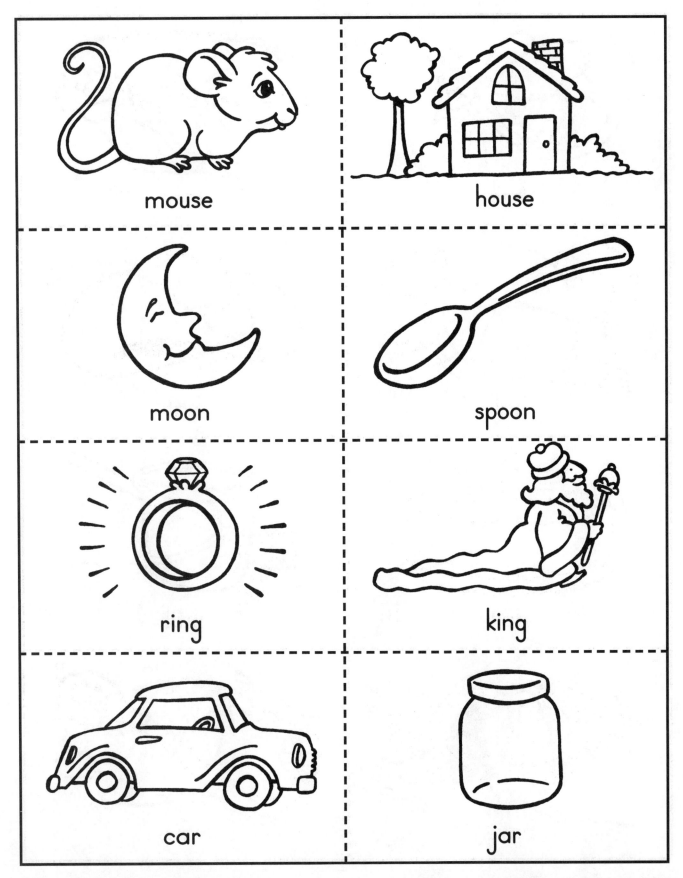

mouse

house

moon

spoon

ring

king

car

jar

Rhyming Practice Cards *(cont.)*

tail

snail

ball

wall

nail

pail

cave

wave

Rhyming Practice Cards *(cont.)*

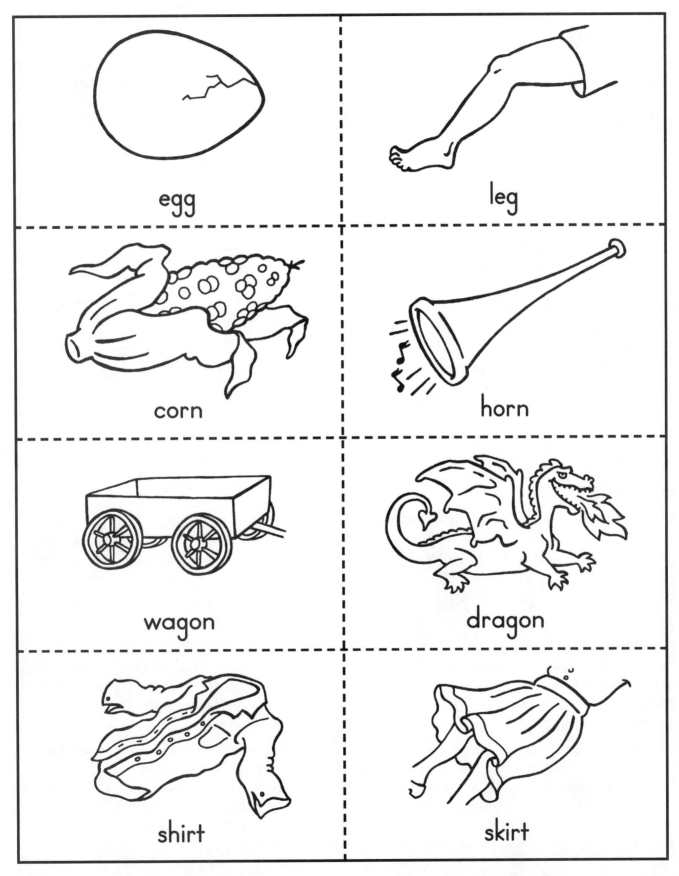

egg

leg

corn

horn

wagon

dragon

shirt

skirt

Syllables

WHAT

A *syllable* is a segment of speech consisting of a vowel with or without one or more accompanying consonant sounds. The words *I* and *snow* are each one syllable long. The words *myself* and *snowman* are each two syllables long. This lesson focuses on syllables. It introduces the concept of syllables and how different words have different numbers of syllables.

WHY

Although the ability to define and pick out syllables is not a skill tested or needed at preschool age, activities that involve syllables can be highly stimulating for children. Preschool children are at a stage of development where they are becoming aware of the power of language and words. They are learning new vocabulary at a phenomenal rate. The introduction of syllables can stimulate children to think about word length and how words are constructed. Syllable games focus on a child learning to:

- listen carefully
- increase vocabulary
- coordinate gross motor skills (clapping) to sound
- coordinate tactile movements (feeling one's chin on one's hand) to sound
- develop an awareness of word uniqueness and length
- practice counting skills
- develop a framework for higher-level tasks such as spelling and an awareness of where a word can be broken at the end of a line during writing

HOW

Engage children in a discussion where one asks what words they think are longer or bigger. To do this, a teacher might have two children repeat their names and compare them. He or she can also introduce two words, such as *dinosaur* and *mouse*, *bike* and *bicycle*, *plane* and *airplane*, *snow* and *snowman*, *rain* and *raindrop*.

At this point, the teacher should bring up words that don't sound bigger or smaller than each other. He or she might want to ask the question, "Do these words sound the same size, or does one sound bigger than the other?" Word pairs might be *school* and *pool*, *rat* and *cat*, *house* and *mouse*, *sing* and *thing*.

After assuring children that some words are longer or bigger than others, while others are shorter or smaller than others, explain that words can be broken down into syllables—chunks of sound. Each word has a certain number of syllables, and we can count them. Have children repeat the word *syllable* several times. Ask them if they think the word has a lot of syllables or a few.

Have each child put one hand under his or her chin. Tell the child that he or she is going to count the number of times his or her chin moves his or her hand when saying the word *syllable*. Slowly and clearly, and with exaggerated movements, say the word *syllable*. Ask children how many times their chins hit their hands (*three*). Repeat this several times until the children agree that it is three. A teacher may want to hold up one of his or her hands and put up one finger every time a syllable is spoken so the children receive a visual reinforcement of the count.

Syllables *(cont.)*

HOW *(cont.)*

Repeat this activity with an assortment of words, perhaps starting with children's names. Also the following is a list of fun words with which to begin.

elephant (3)	jump (1)	lion (2)
cat (1)	jumping (2)	boy (1)
girl (1)	kangaroo (3)	sun (1)

A teacher may choose to have picture cards of the words so that children can begin to associate written word length with spoken word length. This activity can be done throughout the school year. As new units and themes are covered, new vocabulary words can be analyzed for how many syllables they contain.

At some point, a teacher may want to point out to children that the number of syllables a word contains has nothing to do with the actual size of the object to which the word refers. For example,

"In real life, a house is bigger than a mouse. Is *house* bigger than *mouse* when we are counting syllables?"

"In real life, a car is bigger than a jar. Is *car* bigger than *jar* when we are counting syllables?"

"In real life, a snake is bigger than an ant. Is *snake* bigger than *ant* when we are counting syllables?"

An alternative way of counting syllables is to "clap" them. Instead of one putting one's hand underneath one's chin, one claps once for every syllable. A teacher may choose to incorporate this method at the same time as the hand beneath the chin, or wait for a different day. For this method, the teacher would follow the same steps as the hand method and use the same words. This method relies more on hearing rather than touch. Together, the two exercises reinforce each other. Some children will prefer one method to the other.

HANDS-ON PRACTICE

Provide children with copies of pictures to color (pages 81–86). Have them order each card according to number of syllables in the word. The pictures can be pasted in order on a larger sheet of paper. A teacher may choose to couple this activity with number recognition and have children write or paste corresponding numbers next to the animal pictures. (Use the number cards on page 179.)

CLASS EXTENSION

Find a children's dictionary and show children how words are divided into syllables in the dictionary.

HOME PAGE

Hello,

Today we talked about *syllables*. We discussed how words can be broken down into syllables, and that some words have more syllables than others. We combined counting syllables with physical movement.

This activity develops a child's awareness of word length while encouraging a child to listen carefully. It develops a framework for higher-level school tasks such as spelling and knowing where a word can be broken at the end of a line during writing.

Asking your child how many syllables words contain is a great way to engage him or her while driving in a car or waiting in line. Ask your child how many syllables there are in family names or on the words spotted on signs and storefronts.

Use the hand under the chin and/or the clapping method.

Hand Under Chin
- Put your hand underneath your chin.
- Slowly and clearly pronounce the word.
- Count the number of times your chin hits your hand.

Clapping Method
- Clap each syllable.
- Count the number of claps.

Have fun!

Syllable Practice Cards

cat

monkey

elephant

alligator

hippopotamus

lion

Syllable Practice Cards *(cont.)*

snake

giraffe

octopus

rhinoceros

anteater

skunk

Syllable Practice Cards *(cont.)*

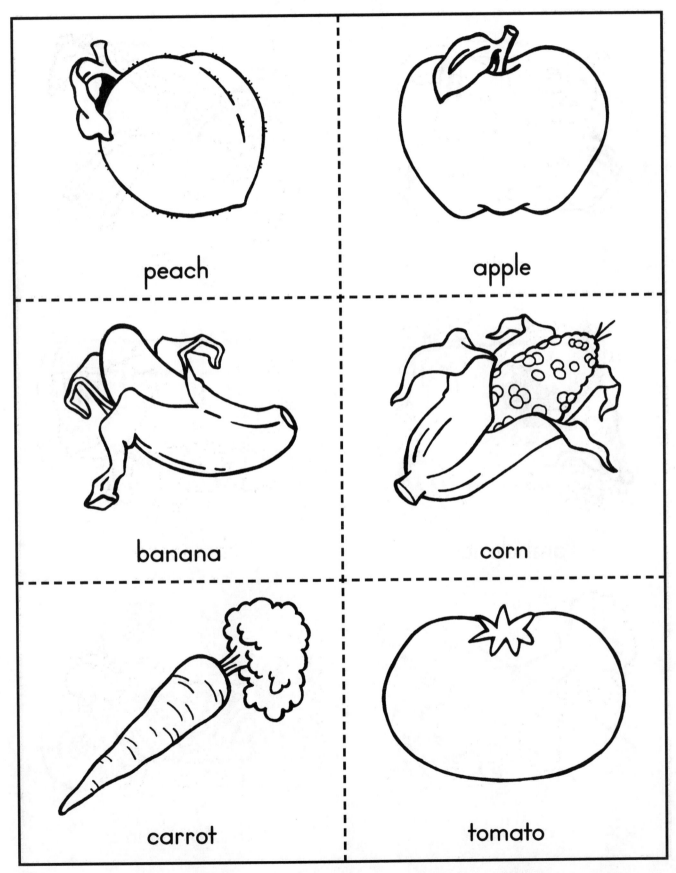

peach

apple

banana

corn

carrot

tomato

Syllable Practice Cards *(cont.)*

car

tractor

ambulance

bus

airplane

motorcycle

Syllable Practice Cards *(cont.)*

girl

boy

notebook

ruler

calculator

pencil

Syllable Practice Cards (cont.)

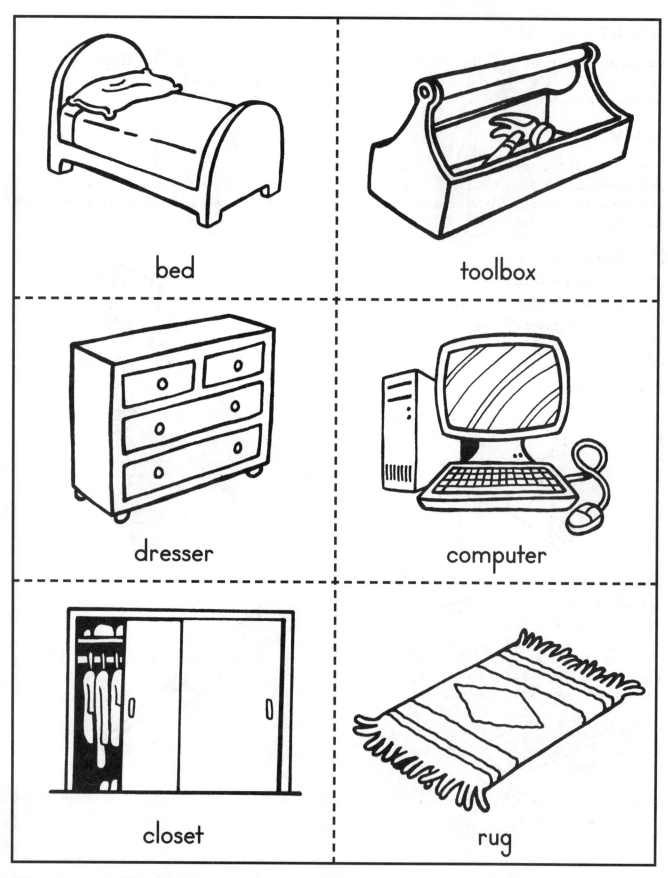

bed

toolbox

dresser

computer

closet

rug

Vowels

WHAT

One of the rules of the English language is that words must contain vowels. Our vowels are "a," "e," "i," "o," and "u." The letter "y" sometimes acts as a vowel in words such as *by* and *my*. This activity focuses on introducing vowels to students and the rule that all words contain them.

WHY

While it is true that many preschool children are not at a stage of development where they can understand and use phonics rules, familiarizing children with the vowel names and consonant names provides a strong foundation for reading success later on. Introducing vowels will help a child with the following:

- visual discrimination
- familiarity with the letters of the alphabet designated as vowels
- familiarity with the rule that every word must contain a vowel
- written language skills

HOW

First, lead students in a sing-song repetition of the vowels.

A, E, I, O, U!
A, E, I, O, U!
A, E,
A, E,
A, E,
A, E,
A, E, I, O, U!

Second, explain that "a," "e," "i," "o," and "u" are special letters of the alphabet. They are vowels, and every word has to have a vowel.

Next, to associate the name of the vowel with its letter representative, hold up cards with the vowels printed on them as the names are spoken. A set of vowel cards is provided (pages 90–91), and a teacher may choose to laminate a set for himself or herself.

At this point, or at any other time during the lesson or day, a teacher may incorporate a physical release into the lesson by having children recite the alphabet. When a vowel is spoken, the children jump up, clap their hands, or shout, etc.

Another way to incorporate physical movement is to have the children draw the called-out vowels in the air, trace them on their palms, bottom of feet, foreheads, or on the backs of classmates.

Vowels *(cont.)*

HOW *(cont.)*

Engage children in a question and answer game in which the teacher or a child calls out,

"I have an 'A.' Is it a vowel?"   "I have an 'X.' Is it a vowel?"

A variation may be that a teacher or a child points to or holds up a letter and calls out, "Is this letter a vowel?"

Embark on a Vowel Search and Discover Mission in which children have to find the vowels the teacher is holding up or calling out somewhere in the classroom, or they have to find all the vowels in the printed words decorating the classroom.

HANDS-ON PRACTICE

Children may color or trace copies of the vowel cards (pages 90–91). Use both the uppercase and lowercase letters if desired. Children can match these cards, as well as use them for reference when they search for vowels. For example, they can be given a page with words printed on it and asked to circle, box, or underline the vowels (see pages 92–93). Also, they can be provided with a list of all the names of the children in the class and directed to circle the vowels in each name. They can then be asked what name contains the most vowels.

If a particular theme or unit is being covered that day, children can be asked to find the vowels in words that pertain to the theme. This type of hands-on practice, as well as the singing of the vowel song (see page 87), can be repeated throughout the year to add an extra dimension to each unit.

CLASS EXTENSIONS

Have children open a favorite book. Send them on a Vowel Search and Discover Mission where they have to find one of each vowel name.

If more gross motor activity is needed, have children try to form the vowel shape with their entire bodies.

You can also have children search for vowels on the Home Page (page 89) that is sent home to parents. Children can mark the page, showing their caregivers what they have learned.

HOME PAGE

Hello,

Today we talked about the vowels "a," "e," "i," "o," and "u." We worked on naming and identifying vowels, as well as finding vowel letters in different words.

These activities help a child develop visual discrimination. They provide familiarity with the letters of the alphabet designated as vowels and with the rule that every word contains a vowel. These types of exercises will facilitate reading advancement later on.

Engage your child in Vowel Search and Discovery Missions. Ask him or her to find the vowels on road signs and store names (if driving) or on cereal and other food boxes (if at home).

We sang,

A, E, I, O, U!
A, E, I, O, U!
A, E,
A, E,
A, E,
A, E,
A, E, I, O, U!

Have fun!

Vowel Practice Cards

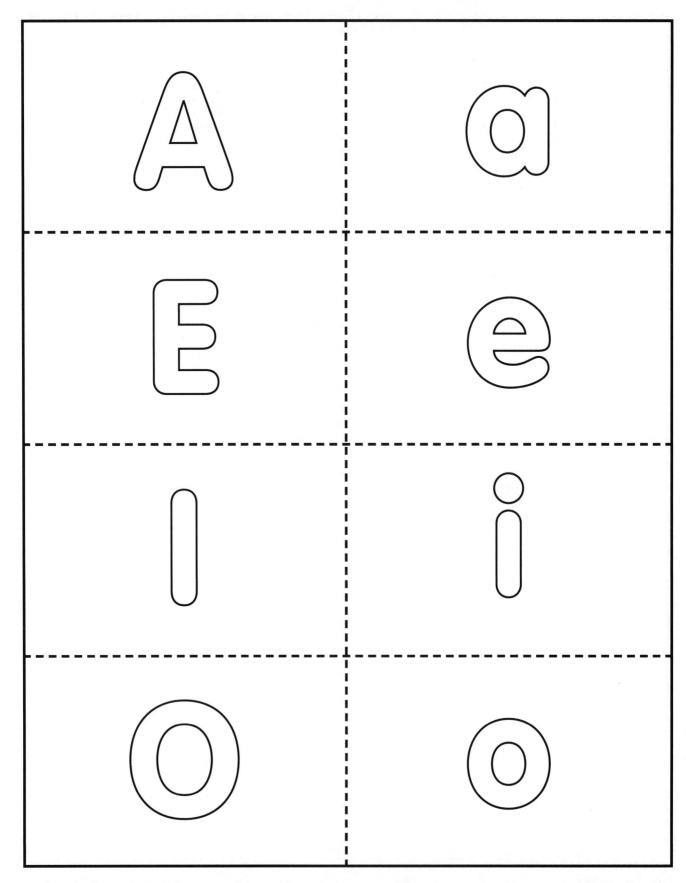

Name _____

Vowel Practice *(cont.)*

Circle the vowels.

Nouns

WHAT

A *noun* is a word that is the name of a person, place, or thing. This lesson focuses on identifying and classifying a noun as a person, place, or thing.

WHY

Children will be required to identify parts of speech as they advance in school. Although nouns are not typically introduced into preschool curriculum, activities with nouns can be easily included. Children of preschool age are at a developmental stage where they are busy sorting and classifying (what is big, small, male, female, old, young, etc.). Extending this type of interest into noun-related activities:

- increases vocabulary
- provides familiarity with nouns
- provides practice sorting words in a new way
- develops reasoning skills
- provides a building block for grammar exercises required at higher grade levels

HOW

Engage children in a discussion about nouns by first bringing up a name, a place, and a thing. A teacher might want to use the name of a child in the class, a place that everyone is aware of (such as the city or classroom the children are in), and a thing that the children can see and touch (such as a chair, window, book, or stuffed animal).

Next, tell the children that all three things are related in a special way. A teacher might want to have children guess how these things are related. Children might bring up color and size. Regardless of whether or not children can find a connection among the three things, the teacher should compliment them on their thinking skills and say, "You didn't know the word I wanted, but your ideas were great. Very good thinking. The connection I wanted was that they were all *nouns*—a word I am guessing you have never heard before."

At this point, have the children say the word *noun* several times. It can be done in sets of five and spoken quickly, slowly, loudly, and softly. It can be pronounced in a silly voice, or, if the class needs a physical release, cried out as they jump or run in place. Depending on the level of the class, and what activities have been done before, a teacher might want to have the children count the number of letters and syllables in the word *noun*, as well as identify the vowels. They can also identify beginning and ending sounds and write the letters in the air.

Next, explain that a *noun* is a person, place, or thing. Go back to the three items talked about at the beginning of the lesson. One by one, state the name and then have children decide if it is a person, place, or thing.

| Person | Place | Thing |

Nouns *(cont.)*

HOW *(cont.)*

Finally, have children behave as Noun Detectives where they have to decide if a noun is a person, place, or thing. A possible list of nouns might be

cat

car

cartoon

name of a child

banana

juice

name of a city

name of a state

teacher's name

name of the school

hat

shoe

swimming pool

name of an adult

book

Nouns		
Person	**Place**	**Thing**
Cole	Indiana	corn
Terra	closet	mouse
mom		tractor
teacher		

A variation of this exercise is to have children provide a noun word. Classmates then have to decide if the named noun is a person, place, or thing. When this game is first introduced, children will often make mistakes when it comes to providing a noun on their own. If a child suggests a word like *sing*, for example, a teacher should not say, "Wrong." Instead, he or she should redirect by saying, "Good word. *Sing* is actually what we call a verb—an action word. But now I know you can come up with the name of a person (or place or thing)" or "Is that a person? No. Is that a place? No. Is that a thing? No. It is a good word, but I think you can come up with another one that is a noun."

HANDS-ON PRACTICE

Make copies for each child of the Noun Practice pages (pages 97–100). Have children circle each type of noun with the appropriate color.

CLASS EXTENSION

Using a familiar book or story, ask children to identify some nouns. Ask them for characters' names, places mentioned, and some things talked about in the book.

HOME PAGE

Hello,

Today we talked about nouns. *Nouns* are words that name a person, place, or thing.

This activity provides familiarity with nouns and increases a child's vocabulary. It provides practice in sorting words in a new way. It also serves as a building block for grammar exercises required later on at higher grade levels.

Entertain your child and fill in waiting time by asking him or her about nouns. Call out a noun and ask your child to be a Noun Detective. Is the noun a person, place, or thing? Use nouns from what is happening around you, as well as from television shows and books.

Have your child name a noun. Then, you answer if the said noun is a person, place, or thing. This is a more difficult task for a child, and a child might say a different type of word. If this happens, say, "Is that a person? No. Is that a place? No. Is it a thing? No. I think you have to come up with another word."

Have fun!

Name _____

Noun Practice

Make a blue circle around each person.

Make a red circle around each place.

Make a black circle around each thing.

Name _____

Noun Practice *(cont.)*

Make a blue circle around each person.

Make a red circle around each place.

Make a black circle around each thing.

Name _____

Noun Practice *(cont.)*

Make a blue circle around each person.

Make a red circle around each place.

Make a black circle around each thing.

Name _____

Noun Practice *(cont.)*

Make a blue circle around each person.

Make a red circle around each place.

Make a black circle around each thing.

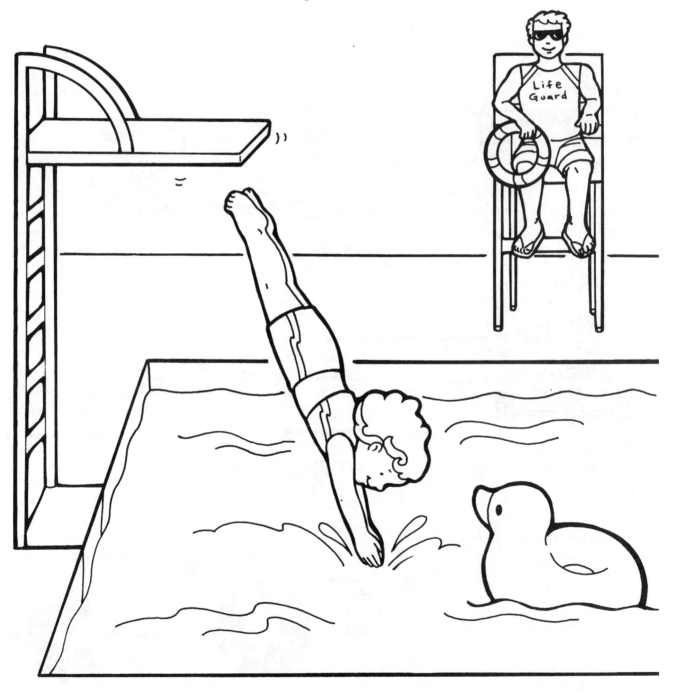

Adjectives

WHAT

An *adjective* is a word that describes a noun or pronoun. It tells which, what kind of, how many, or whose. In the phrase, *the big, round ball, big* and *round* are adjectives. In the sentence, *He is a good boy, good* is an adjective. This lesson focuses on identifying and naming adjectives.

WHY

Children will be required to identify parts of speech as they advance in school. Although adjectives are not typically introduced in preschool curriculum, activities with adjectives can be easily included. Children of preschool age are at a developmental stage where they are busy sorting and classifying. They want answers to questions that focus on which, what kind of, how many, and whose. Extending this type of interest into adjective-related activities increases vocabulary by:

- providing familiarity with adjectives
- providing practice sorting words in a new way
- developing reasoning skills
- providing a building block for grammar exercises required at higher grade levels

HOW

Before beginning this lesson, a teacher may want to write the word *adjective* on a piece of paper or the board for a visual prompt. In addition, a teacher may want to have several pictures that are easily described. For example, people wearing clothes of specific colors, an assortment of animals, cars, or food.

Begin the lesson by holding up the flashcard with the word *adjective* printed on it. Explain that today everyone is going to figure out what adjectives are. Tell the children that they will start being Adjective Detectives in a minute, but first they have to get their mouths and their ears used to the word *adjective*.

Hold up the card with the word *adjective* on it so that children can see it. Have them repeat the word slowly, enunciating clearly and exaggerating mouth movements. Then, have them speak it at a normal speed.

Next, tell the children that they are ready to be Adjective Detectives. Tell them that adjectives are words that describe people, places, or things. They tell which, what kind of, how many, or whose. Some of the children may look confused, but assure them not to worry. Tell them it gets easy with practice.

To start, hold up a picture or point to something someone is wearing. Describe what you are pointing to with a simple sentence such as, "Ty's shirt is blue." Say the sentence again with a pause between each word so that each word is distinctive. Then ask, "What word in the sentence 'Ty's shirt is blue' describes what kind of shirt it is?" If children are not able to come up with the word *blue*, lead them to it by saying, "Is the shirt red? Oh, it's blue! So *blue* tells me what kind of shirt it is. Blue is the adjective."

Adjectives *(cont.)*

HOW *(cont.)*

Some sample sentences might be:

"I have two hands." *(two)*

"A lion has four paws." *(four)*

"I have one nose." *(one)*

"The red ball rolled away." *(red)*

"The black cat had four kittens." *(black, four)*

"The big, green frog jumped." *(big, green)*

Hold up some of your pictures or point to objects in the classroom and ask children to come up with some adjectives that describe them. Help them put their adjectives into proper sentences.

If a physical release is needed, have children squat down while you say a sentence. Give them a moment to figure out what the adjective is, leading them to it if necessary. (For example, if your sentence is, "I have two strong legs," you might lead children to the right answer by saying, "Remember, an adjective would tell us what our legs are like.") Then, repeat the sentence slowly and have the children jump when you say the adjectives *two* and *strong*.

As a final exercise, a teacher can put an object in the middle of the circle. Have children take turns coming up with adjectives to describe it. If, for example, a book is put in the middle, children can describe it as *hard, small, colored, pretty, good, boring, silly, funny, one,* etc.

HANDS-ON PRACTICE

Make a tally of how many children fit these adjective phrases.

- children with black hair
- children with blond hair
- children with brown hair
- children with red hair

- children with two feet
- children with three feet
- children with happy faces
- children with sad faces

- children with four-legged pets
- children with big brothers or big sisters
- children with little brothers or little sisters

CLASS EXTENSIONS

Take a character from a familiar book or nursery rhyme. Have children use adjectives to describe the character.

Play a game in which the teacher uses adjectives to describe an unnamed student or a character in a book. The students have to guess who it is. For example, a teacher may look at a student and say, "He has black hair. He has two eyes. His pants are long and blue. His red shirt is short-sleeved. His eyes are green. He is a fast runner. He is a good tree climber."

If a teacher is using a character out of a book, such as Jack from *Jack and the Beanstalk*, adjective use might go like this: "He is a fast runner because he had to run away. He is a good climber because he had to climb up a big, green bean stalk."

HOME PAGE

Hello,

Today we talked about adjectives. *Adjectives* are words that describe nouns or pronouns. In the sentence, "The furry dog has one tail," the words *furry* and *one* are adjectives. They describe the dog and the tail.

This activity provides familiarity with adjectives and increases a child's vocabulary. It gives your child practice in sorting words in a new way. It also serves as a building block for grammar exercises required later on at higher grade levels.

Entertain your child and fill in waiting time by asking him or her about adjectives. Ask your child to describe objects or people he or she sees. Or, if your child is having a difficult time coming up with adjectives, direct him or her by asking, "Is the car in front of us white or blue? What color is the adjective we want?"

Play a game in which your child is an Adjective Detective. Say simple sentences that include an adjective such as, "You have pretty hair," "You are a fast runner," or "I see a bike with three wheels." Then, ask your child which words in the sentences were adjectives. If he or she needs to be directed, lead your child to the answer by asking which word described hair, told what type of runner he or she is, or how many wheels something had.

Have fun!

Verb Endings

WHAT

Verbs are action words like *run, swim,* and *eat*. Sometimes, when there are different subjects such as *I, he,* or *we,* the verb has a slightly different ending. For example, an "s" is added to *run* when it is coupled with *he*. *I run, he runs,* and *we run*. This lesson focuses on different verb endings.

WHY

Children are at the age when their vocabularies are expanding everyday. They are learning grammar by listening to and repeating what they hear around them. By actively engaging children in exercises where one focuses on verb endings, one:

- reinforces the idea of subject-verb agreement
- helps to increase their vocabulary
- offer practice with past, present, and future tenses
- provides an introduction to grammatical exercises later required in school

HOW

Engage children in a verbal exchange in which they respond orally to your prompts. An example of an exchange could involve the verb *run*. Point to yourself, and say, "I run." Point to a boy and say, "He runs." Next, point to a girl, and say, "She runs." Make a motion that includes the entire circle and say, "We run." Point to two or three children and say, "They run." Point to another child and say, "You run." Mix in names of the children in singular and plural combinations, too.

Ask children if most of the time the words sounded the same. Tell them that though it is often just a little sound that makes the verbs different when you use them with different subjects, the sound is needed and very important. If the sound is forgotten, it is like getting dressed but having your pants on inside out. It is like wearing shoes that don't match. It just doesn't sound right.

Once children understand what it is you want them to respond with, continue with verbs like these:

clap	jump	smile
color	laugh	snore
dress	paint	swim
eat	ride	walk
hop	sleep	yawn

To help children release energy and keep them focused, one might want to couple physical actions with the exchanges. For example, when one says, "I sleep," one might want to act out putting his or her head down and sleeping.

Verb Endings *(cont.)*

HOW *(cont.)*

When children can handle this activity with ease, tell them that they have gotten so good that it is now too easy. To make it harder, you are going to make them think about when things happen—today, tomorrow, or yesterday.

Begin a discussion in which you ask what the difference is between these three words. Then, point to yourself and say, "Yesterday, I ran. Today, I run. Tomorrow, I will run." Continue as you did before, with different subjects (*he, she, you, we,* and *they,* as well as the names of children in the class) and verbs (those listed below as well as any others you desire).

This activity can be repeated throughout the school year. It can be especially relevant when new vocabulary words are introduced.

Here is a list of some common irregular verbs:

Present	Past	Present	Past
begin	began	blow	blew
break	broke	bring	brought
choose	chose	come	came
do	did	draw	drew
drink	drank	drive	drove
eat	ate	fall	fell
fly	flew	forget	forgot
freeze	froze	get	got
give	gave	go	went
grow	grew	ride	rode
run	ran	see	saw
speak	spoke	swim	swam
swing	swung	take	took
throw	threw	wear	wore

Verb Endings *(cont.)*

HANDS-ON PRACTICE

Make a copy of Verb Endings Practice (pages 108–110) for each child. First, practice using the verb *wear*. A teacher might point to himself or herself and say, "Yesterday, I wore blue pants and a white shirt; Today I wear red pants and a green shirt; Tomorrow, I will wear an orange skirt and a red shirt." Next, the teacher will color in the blank outline with what he or she wore yesterday, today, as well as what the teacher thinks he or she will wear tomorrow.

A teacher might want to ask each child, one-by-one, what he or she is wearing and wore yesterday. Many children (as well as the teacher!) might not remember, but with the group's help, memories might be stirred. If a child cannot remember even with help, tell the child that he or she can make up the outfit.

Next, have children color in what they wore yesterday, today, and what they might wear tomorrow on the three outlines. If a teacher wants, he or she can save the copy of what the children colored of what they might wear tomorrow. The next day, the class can compare the picture to what the child is actually wearing.

CLASS EXTENSION

Introduce the "ing" form. Say, "Yesterday, I sat. Today, I sit. Tomorrow I will sit. Right now I am sitting." Make the motion of physically sitting down to emphasize the present state.

These are some other verbs that work well for this activity:

- run: Yesterday, I ran. Today, I run. Tomorrow, I will run. Right now I am running.
  (Run in place to emphasize the present state.)

- jump: Yesterday, I jumped. Today, I jump. Tomorrow, I will jump. Right now I am jumping.
  (Jump in place to emphasize the present state.)

- clap

- eat

- wiggle

- laugh

- cry

- stretch

- stand

HOME PAGE

Hello,

Today we talked about verb endings. We practiced putting the right ending on verbs like *eat, swim,* and *run.* For example,

I eat, he eats, she eats, you eat, they eat, and we eat.

I swim, he swims, she swims, you swim, they swim, and we swim.

I run, he runs, she runs, you run, they run, and we run.

We also extended this activity to verb tenses. We added in the words *yesterday, today,* and *tomorrow.* For example,

Yesterday, I ate. Today, I eat. Tomorrow, I will eat.

Yesterday, I swam. Today, I swim. Tomorrow, I will swim.

Yesterday, I ran. Today, I run. Tomorrow, I will run.

This particular exercise was also done with the subjects *he, she, you, we,* and *they.* For example,

Yesterday, he ate. Today, he eats. Tomorrow, he will eat.

Yesterday, she swam. Today, she swims. Tomorrow, she will swim.

Yesterday, they ran. Today, they run. Tomorrow, they will run.

This activity provides children with an introduction to tenses, as well as subject-verb agreement.

Engage your child in fun question-and-answer sessions where you say, "I (any verb, such as *run*). He _____. (*runs*) She _____." (*runs*) Or questions that involve tense, such as "Yesterday, I _____ (*any verb, such as drank*). Today, I _____. (*drink*) Tomorrow I will _____." (*drink*)

Have fun!

Name _____

Verb Endings Practice
What I Wore Yesterday

Color in what you wore
yesterday on this picture.

Name _____

Verb Endings Practice *(cont.)*

What I Wear Today

Color in what you wear
today on this picture.

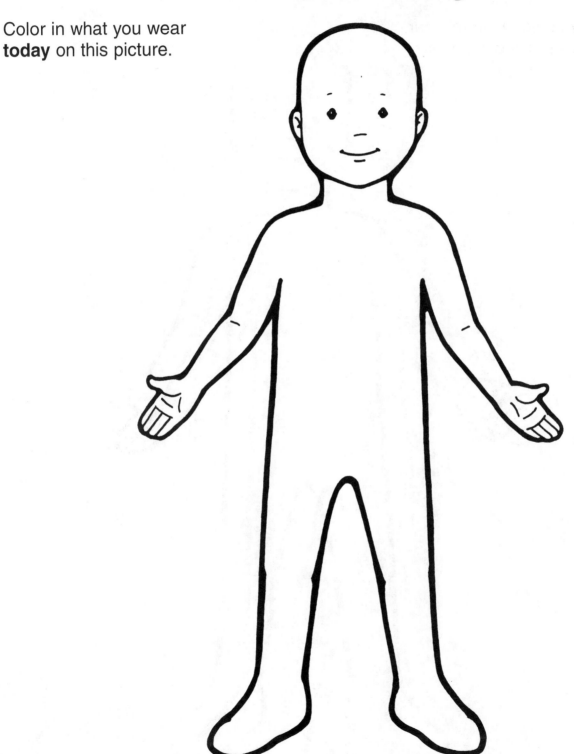

Name _____

Verb Endings Practice (cont.)

What I Will Wear Tomorrow

Color in what you plan to wear **tomorrow** on this picture.

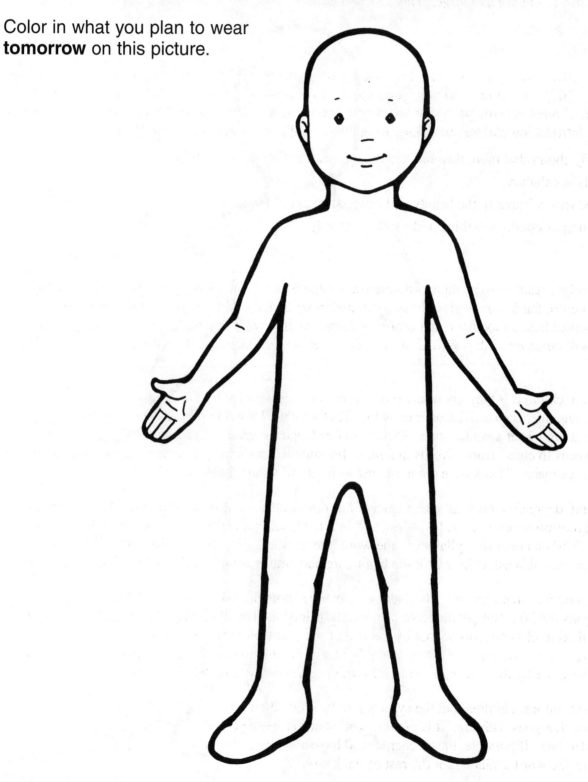

110

Synonyms

WHAT

Synonyms are words that have the same or almost the same meaning as other words. *Little* and *small* are synonyms, as are *big* and *large*. This lesson focuses on the identification and use of synonyms.

WHY

Preschool children are at a stage where their language skills are still developing. Their vocabularies are increasing. They are figuring out how language works, by listening and with trial and error attempts. Sometimes, if rules or basic processes are clearly presented, children can understand more fully what is going on. Introducing children to synonyms and having them actively work with them:

- clearly shows that more than one word may mean almost the same thing
- builds vocabulary
- introduces children to the beauty and expressiveness of language
- encourages children to think and speak creatively

HOW

A teacher might want to write the word *synonym* on the board or on a large piece of paper to use as a visual aid before the lesson begins. Start a discussion by naming some things that are often described as big (a school bus, a mountain, an ocean). Ask the children what size the objects are. Hopefully, the word *big* will come up in the discussion. If it does not, lead children to it by asking, "Is an ocean big or small?"

Next, ask the children if they know any other words they can use for *big* (*large, giant, not small, huge, enormous, gigantic, colossal*). Continue with, "That's right. There are lots of ways we can say something is big. That's what makes talking and our language great. It's never boring because we have so many words to chose from. Words that have the same or almost the same meaning as other words are called *synonyms*. That's what we are going to focus on today—synonyms."

At this point, depending on what else a teacher has done, a teacher may want to have the children say the word *synonym* several times, fast, slow, and in a loud, soft, and silly voice. In addition, a teacher may have children count the syllables in the word, the number of letters, and the number of vowels. The teacher may also ask children for the beginning and ending sounds and write the letters in the air.

Explain to children that they may not know very many synonyms. For example, they may not know all the synonyms for *big*. But people learn new words as long as they live! What the class is going to be doing is thinking of synonyms so that by the end of the year everyone knows many more synonyms. Remind the children that they may not remember them the first time they hear them, or the second, or even the third, but by the end of the year, they will begin to recognize them.

At this point, inform children that the synonym to be worked on for today is one that goes with *big*. It is *gigantic* (or whatever word you have decided on). If possible, the teacher should have a large flashcard of the word available for the rest of the lesson.

Synonyms *(cont.)*

HOW *(cont.)*

A teacher may want to have the children take turns naming something that is gigantic or answering questions about whether or not something is big and gigantic.

Many teachers may be thinking that these words are beyond their students. Children should not be tested on these words or expected to learn them all. At the same time, it cannot be stressed enough that words should not be excluded because they seem too difficult. What this lesson does is introduce to a child the *possibilities* of language. Some children will remember all of these words. Other children will not, but they will have practiced articulating sounds and other word details. They will understand that they have choices when it comes to words.

This is the type of lesson that should be interspersed with other activities all year. There should be some set times to learn a synonym, perhaps once a week, where the word is repeated so many times, vowels and syllables counted, etc. Then, during the week, reinforce the word by having children repeat it a few times. If children describe something as big later during the year, the teacher can stop and say, "Big. What is another word we can use for *big*?"

These are some words that can be used for synonym lessons:

- *big*—large, giant, great, gigantic, enormous, huge, colossal
- *small*—tiny, minute, miniature, undersized, petite
- *perfect*—ideal, just right, impeccable
- *funny*—humorous, comic, witty, silly, not serious
- *fast*—quick, speedy, rapid, swift, hasty, prompt
- *slow*—sluggish, unhurried, dawdling
- *car*—automobile, vehicle
- *fantastic*—incredible, unbelievable, extraordinary, out of this world
- *talkative*—garrulous, chatty (Children giggle at being told, "Oh, everyone is talking too much today. Everyone is garrulous!)

HANDS-ON PRACTICE

Practice will vary depending on what word is introduced. One suggestion is to have a sheet of paper with two synonyms, such as *big* and *gigantic*, printed on it. Children can trace the words. Or, children can draw something that fits the word. In the case of *big* and *gigantic*, for example, they can draw something big.

CLASS EXTENSION

Look up the two synonyms in the dictionary. Read the definitions aloud. Have the children listen to see if the synonyms are used in the definitions.

HOME PAGE

Hello,

Today we talked about synonyms. *Synonyms* are words that have the same or almost the same meaning as another word. *Little* and *small* are synonyms, as are *big* and *large*. This activity helps build a child's vocabulary. It introduces him or her to the notion that words are related and that many words can mean the same thing. It is this type of activity that encourages a child to think and speak creatively. Engage your child in synonym games by encouraging him or her to come up with words that mean nearly the same thing. For example, If you see something that is big, say, "That's really big. No, it's not just big, it's big and . . . . (huge) No, it's not just big and huge, it's . . . . (gigantic)."

Your child may prefer games where he or she chooses a synonym. For example, if your child does something well, you can say, "Oh, good job. Yes, a very good job. So if it's a good job, is it a tiny job or a perfect job? So if it's a good and perfect job, is it an ideal job or a sad job?"

If you want a child to do something quickly, you might say, "I want you to go fast! So if I want you to go fast, do I want you to go hastily or slowly? If I want you go fast and with haste, do I want you to go rapidly or crawling? If I want you to go hastily, rapidly, and fast, do I want you to go quickly or sleepily?"

Every family will have its favorite synonyms. These are some of the ones we will be using in class:

- big—large, giant, great, gigantic, enormous, huge, colossal
- small—tiny, minute, miniature, undersized, petite
- perfect—ideal, just right, impeccable
- funny—humorous, comic, witty, silly, not serious
- fast—quick, speedy, rapid, swift, hasty, prompt
- slow—sluggish, unhurried, dawdling
- car—automobile, vehicle
- fantastic—incredible, unbelievable, extraordinary, out of this world
- talkative—garrulous, chatty (Children giggle at being told, "Oh, everyone is talking too much today. Everyone is garrulous.")

Have fun!

Analogies

WHAT

An *analogy* is a likeness in some ways or a comparision between things that are otherwise unlike. Exercises with analogies deal with finding the relationship or the bridge between two words. For example, if one is given the stimulus pair *nose : breathe*, the relationship or bridge between the two words is that you use a nose to breathe. Other words that would fit this analogy are *eyes : see* (you use eyes to see) and *ears : hear* (you use your ears to hear). This exercise focuses on working with analogies by finding the bridge between two stimulus words and then finding other word pairs that fit the same analogy.

WHY

Solving analogies requires recognizing what words mean, as well as applying reasoning skills. Introducing children to analogy exercises at a young age is a fun and interesting way to provide them with exercises in vocabulary and practice in reasoning. In addition, many standardized tests have questions on analogies. By working with analogies now, a child:

- increases vocabulary
- develops reasoning skills
- becomes familiar with standardized test formats
- is introduced to the "playfulness" of language, or a new way that they can think about words

HOW

A teacher may want to print the word *analogy* on a large flashcard before the lesson, as well as make copies of some of the Analogies Practice cards (page 119–122) for use as visual prompts.

Begin the lesson by holding up a picture of a shoe. Ask children what it is, and then articulate clearly that it is a shoe. Next, hold up the picture of a foot. Ask children what it is, making sure that the word *foot* is articulated clearly. Then, hold the cards up and say, "The word *shoe* and the word *foot* are not the same. They represent two very different things. But they are connected in some way. It is as if there is a bridge between them, connecting them. How do they fit together?" If children do not come up with, "You wear a shoe on your foot," or, "You put a shoe on your foot," lead them to it by asking, "Where does a shoe go? Does it go on my head? Do I wear it on my nose? Right, it goes on a foot. We put a shoe on a foot. We wear a shoe on a foot. The bridge between *shoe* and *foot* is that we wear a shoe on our foot." Next, hold up the picture of the hand. Go through the same discussion that you did with *shoe*. Once the word is clearly articulated, bring out the picture of the mitten. Once the word *mitten* is clearly articulated, hold up the cards together. Say, as before, "The words *hand* and *mitten* are not the same. They represent two very different things. But they are connected in some way. It is as if there is a bridge between them, connecting them. How do they fit together?" Lead the children, if necessary, to "You wear a mitten on your hand," or, "You put a mitten on your hand."

Next, ask the children if the bridge is the same between *shoe* and *foot* and *mitten* and *hand*. If children do not respond that it is, lead them to it by saying, "You are right in that a shoe is not a mitten and a foot is not a hand. The words are not the same, so good thinking. But the bridge between these words, what makes them alike, is the same. We wear a shoe on a foot, and we wear a mitten on a hand." Emphasize the word *wear* as you speak.

Analogies *(cont.)*

HOW *(cont.)*

Finally, repeat the same exercise and discussion for the analogy pair *hat* and *head*. Make sure that children understand that *hat* and *head* fit the same bridge used to connect *mitten* to *hand* and *shoe* to *foot*.

It is at this point that a teacher can decide to bring up the word *analogy* or not. Becoming familiar with the word *analogy* does not affect the lesson at all. But a teacher may use it to vary the lesson and keep children engaged. Also, many children like things to be named. They like to know exactly what they are doing.

If the word *analogy* is introduced, a teacher should explain that there is a special word for what they are looking for. There is a special word for the bridge between two words, or what connects them. That word is *analogy*. An *analogy* is a likeness in some way between two words that aren't the same. If a teacher does decide to bring up the word *analogy*, he or she should show the word printed on a card and have children repeat the word about 25 times. It can be repeated in sets of five, with different sets pronouncing the word *analogy* quickly, slowly, loudly, softly, or in a silly voice. The repetitions can be interspersed with activities that have been introduced in class such as counting syllables and numbers of letters in the word, identifying vowels, noting beginning and ending sounds and letters, and writing the word in the air.

It should be noted that the analogies lesson is one that can be done throughout the year. Teachers can reintroduce analogies discussed previously for purposes of familiarity and practice, as well as introduce new ones. Some teachers may choose to pick a specific day of the week for practicing two or three analogies. Other teachers may choose to do one analogy a day. Although this analogies lesson continues, it is up to the teacher how much and how far to push children on any given day.

Continue the lesson with the analogies *hammer : nail* and *screwdriver : screw* (see page 120).

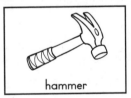
hammer

nail

Lastly, say to the children that they have gotten so good with pictures that now you are going to see if they can solve analogies or find the bridge between two words with just their listening skills. Say the word *nose* very clearly, and have children identify what a nose is. Next, say the word *breathe*. Say to the children, "The analogy is *nose* to *breathe*. *Nose* and *breathe* are two very different words. They mean two very different things. But they are connected in some way. What is the bridge connecting them?" If necessary, lead children to, "You breathe with a nose. You use a nose to breathe."

Next, bring up the analogies *ear : hear;* and *eye : see.* Ask if the same bridge fits with *nose : breathe; ear : hear;* and *eye : see.* Once children have agreed that these three word pairs have the same bridge, ask them if this same bridge fits the one for *shoe : foot.* Ask them if you wear a nail on your hammer. Do they wear a screw on their screwdriver?

As new analogies are worked on throughout the year, bring up old analogies and ask if those analogies have the same bridges as the new ones. This reinforces the different connections between words and acts as a refresher vocabulary lesson.

Analogies *(cont.)*

HOW *(cont.)*

As children become more familiar with analogy exercises, a teacher might want to demonstrate to children how very important order is. For example, *shoe : foot* is very different and not the same as *hand : mitten*. You wear a shoe on your foot. You do not wear a hand on your mitten. Exercises for stressing the importance of word order are easily implemented by giving children one analogy and making sure they are comfortable with it. Then, provide children with sets of words and ask them what fits the same analogy as the first words provided. For example, give children the stimulus words *bear : cub*. (A baby bear is a cub.) Then, ask them which one of the following pairs fits the same bridge, *cow : calf* or *calf : cow*.

This is a list of some analogies that work well for teaching:

Purpose

nose : breathe

ears : hear

eyes : see

Placement

toes : foot

fingers : hand

leaves : tree

rug : floor

picture : wall

Relationships

mom : dad

sister : brother

aunt : uncle

duck : duckling

goose : gosling

pig : piglet

dog : puppy

cat : kitten

Use

chair : sit

bed : sleep

pencil : write

crayon : color

bike : ride

book : read or listen

violin (or other instrument) : play

paintbrush : paint

hoe : weed

Opposites

hot : cold

big : small

tall : short

old : young

Analogies *(cont.)*

HOW *(cont.)*

Because
smile : happy
cry : sad

Time
days : week
weeks : month
months : year
hours : day
minutes : hour
seconds : minute
ten years : decade
100 years : century

Where
boat : ocean (lake, river)
car : road
train : track

HANDS-ON PRACTICE

Make copies of the Analogies Practice (pages 119–122) and cut out the cards. Have children color and match one set of picture pairs to the other set of picture pairs that uses the same analogy bridge. The Animal Families pictures (pages 228–231) work well, too. The adult animals can be paired with the corresponding baby animal.

CLASS EXTENSION

Have one child call out a word. Have another child call out a second word. Engage the children in a discussion where you try to find a relationship or bridge between the two words. Then, try to find another analogy pair that has the same bridge. Be warned that some of these bridges will be outrageous, or they will not work at all! For example, if *motorcycle* and *broccoli* are called out, the bridge might be that you do not want to eat broccoli on a motorcycle, just as you would not want to eat onions in a car.

HOME PAGE

Hello,

Today we did exercises with analogies. We named two unlike words and tried to find a way they were alike.

For example,

> shoe to foot
>
> mitten to hand
>
> hat to head

are all alike in that you wear the first word on the second word.

This activity helps your child build vocabulary as well as develop reasoning skills. He or she has to think about the words, what they mean, and then look for the relationship that somehow bridges them or connects them together.

Engage your child with analogies by asking questions such as,

> "Dog is to puppy as cat is to . . . ." (*kitten*)
>
> "Person is to house as bird is to . . . ." (*nest*)
>
> "Chair is to sit as bed is to . . . ." (*sleep*)

Opposite words are great for this game (hot, cold; big, small; tall, short).

Remember that the order of the words presented can sometimes be very important.

For example,

> smile is to happy as cry is to sad

is not the same as

> smile is to happy as sad is to cry.

Watching for order can add a new dimension to your games.

For example, you can say,

"Fish is to swim.

Does fly is to bird match, or bird is to fly . . . ?" (*bird is to fly*)

Have fun!

Analogies Practice

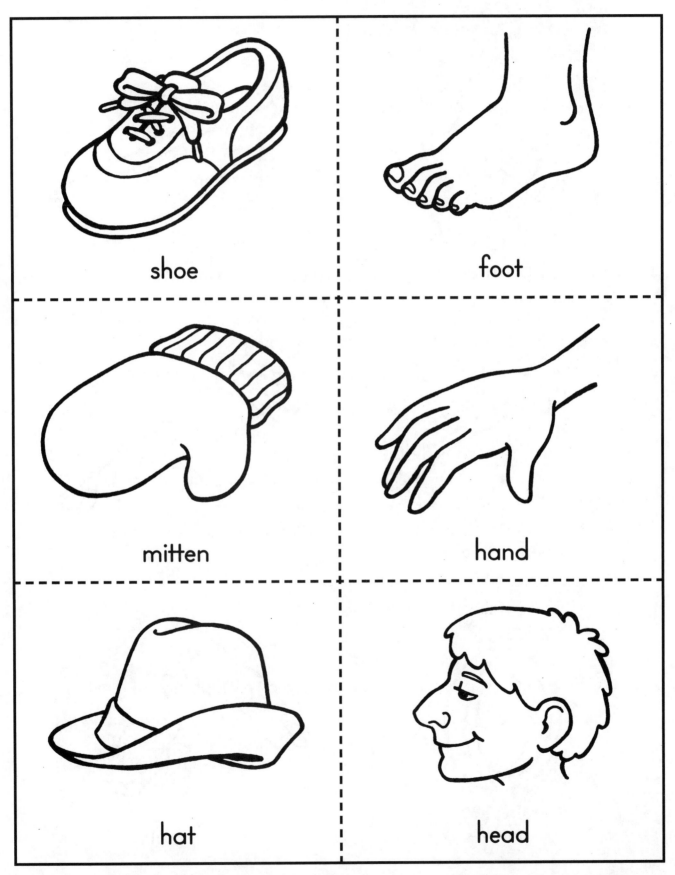

shoe

foot

mitten

hand

hat

head

Analogies Practice *(cont.)*

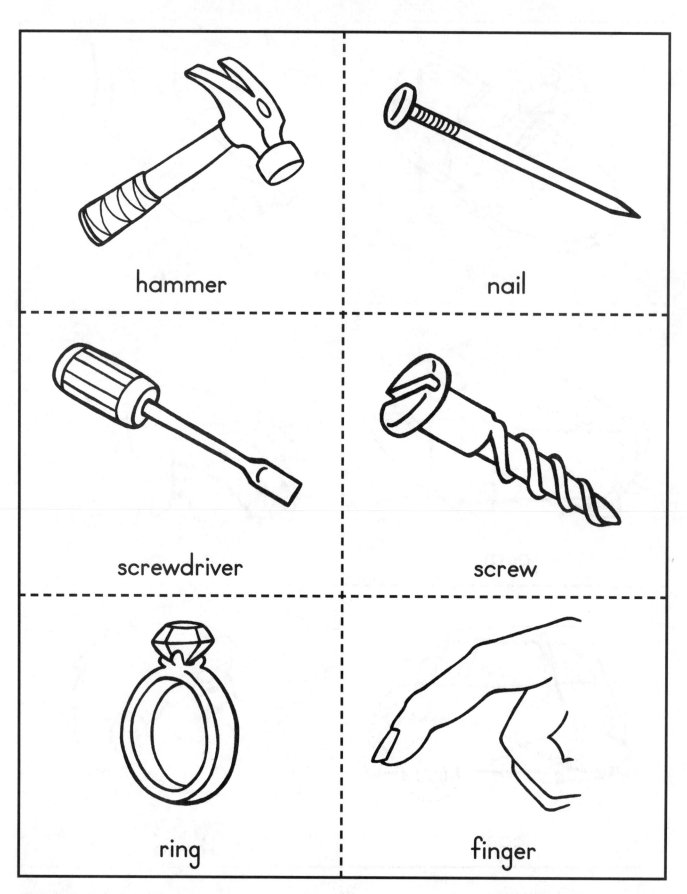

hammer

nail

screwdriver

screw

ring

finger

120

Analogies Practice *(cont.)*

bracelet

arm

boat

ocean

car

road

Analogies Practice *(cont.)*

pencil

paper

chalk

chalkboard

paintbrush

easel

Counting

WHAT

One of the fundamentals of counting is number sequence. *Two* always follows *one* and *three* always follows *two*. This lesson focuses on number sequence and counting from different starting points.

WHY

Counting is a skill so basic that we use it in our daily lives without even thinking about it. Developed counters know that there is a one-to-one correspondence between numbers and objects. One can help develop this maturity by introducing children to counting stretches of numbers. This particular exercise of counting numbers develops a child's:

- familiarity with number names
- understanding of number sequence and progression
- ability to count starting from various points

HOW

The first step is to begin with the numbers zero through ten. Aloud, with children joining in, repeat the sequence 0, 1, 2, 3, 4, 5, 6, 7, 8, 9, 10 several times.

One can add variety by having children repeat this sequence as loudly, quickly, softly, and slowly as they can. As children become more familiar with the numbers, one can even have them shout or whisper every other number.

As proficiency is gained, increase the counting sequence to 15, and then 20. Once 20 is reached, one can count higher in increments of 10.

At some point, a teacher will want to modify his or her request by changing the starting points. For example, ask the children to start at 4 and go to 14; 56 and go to 70; 100 and go to 120; 240 and go to 250; 732 and go to 742; 1,001 and go to 1,025.

If a teacher feels that a physical release should be incorporated, he or she can announce ahead of time, "We are going to count from 25 to 50. As we say the number 45, we are going to jump up (or clap hands, stamp feet). I wonder who will know exactly when to jump?"

This activity can be varied with visual aids. A teacher might point to each number on a large chart as it is recited, or write the numbers that the children will be reciting that day on the board.

Once children begin to gain some mastery over counting, this activity can be used as an entertaining time filler and performed several times a day. While the children are waiting for a drink or to go out to play, they can count from 22 to 33; or 222 to 233.

Counting *(cont.)*

HANDS-ON PRACTICE

Have the children hold their fisted hands out in front of them. Release and hold up one finger as each number is recited until both hands are open and all fingers are out.

Count objects in the room—windows; number of children; shoes; doors; steps one has to take to walk across the room; total number of arms, legs, eyes, and feet that everyone has; etc.

Have children trace the Number Cards (pages 179–185) or copy numbers they have written themselves. When the starting points become more advanced, children can copy numbers from the board, first writing them in the air and then drawing them on a sheet of paper.

CLASS EXTENSIONS

Take it backward! Announce that the children need to perform the countdown for a rocket blastoff. Starting with 10, count down to zero. If the class is enjoying this type of activity, count backward from 20 to 10; 120 to 110; etc.

Line up 11 children shoulder to shoulder, in front of the remaining children. Hand each child in line a number card (not in order) from zero to ten (see pages 179–185). The group of children not in line can direct the children, telling them where to move, until they are in order from zero to ten and from ten to zero. The number of children in line or directing can vary, depending on class size and what a teacher finds manageable with a particular group of children. Also, different numbers can be used with this activity. For example, the children in line can be handed numbers 11–21 or numbers in sequential units like 100–900.

HOME PAGE

Hello,

Today we practiced counting. We started at zero and went up to ten. Over the course of the year, we will count to higher levels and also begin to start our counting at different starting points. For example, we will count from 11 to 21; 44 to 54; etc.

This activity helps a child gain familiarity with number names and understand number sequence and progression.

Entertain your child while driving in a car or waiting somewhere by going on a number search. Look for a one first, and then a two, three, and so on. Use signs, license plates, and highway markers as your hunting grounds.

Request, also, that your child count whenever possible. Different objects can be counted, such as cars, houses, or people one can see. Request a count to your child's age, a count up to 25, or as he or she advances, from various starting points—from 13 to 23; from 26 to 46; or from 172 to 182.

Have fun!

Skip Counting

WHAT

Skip counting, or counting by twos, is when every other number in an ordered sequence is spoken. This patterning activity focuses on teaching children to count by twos, starting at the number one (so the count is 1, 3, 5, 7, 9, etc.) and at the number two (so the count is 2, 4, 6, 8, 10, etc.).

WHY

It takes time and practice for children to develop a one-to-one correspondence with numbers. When children recite the numbers, often it is as if they are reciting a nursery rhyme. They are merely repeating sounds they have heard adults say. Children still do not grasp the cognitive concept of one-to-one correspondence: that each number they name corresponds to a specific amount. When children skip count, they are required to hold or speak a number silently in their heads. Skip counting, as well as other number games and counting activities, helps a child begin to master the concept of one-to-one correspondence. It provides an introduction to or reinforcement of the following ideas:

- there is a one-to-one correspondence between numbers and a specific amount
- numbers are there even when not spoken
- there is a number sequence and progression
- numbers have names
- numbers can be added
- numbers can be multiplied

2 - 4 - 6 - 8 - 10

HOW

A teacher might want to have ready a chart or banner of numbers to refer to as a visual aid. Or, use number cards or a number line where every other card or number can be turned over or crossed out.

Begin by telling children that you are going to count numbers in a very special way. Instead of saying every number aloud, you are only going to say every other number. You are going to say one number, skip the next, and then say a number. Children may not understand what you mean at first, but as you proceed with the lesson, they will begin to understand.

Say "one" very softly, and then say loudly "two." Say "three" softly, and "four" loudly. Continue until 10, 20, or 30, depending on how children are keeping up. If you do have a chart for reference, point to the numbers as they are spoken.

Repeat if needed, or compliment the children and say that it is time to make it a little bit more difficult. This time, tell them that instead of whispering, you will say every other number in your head. Exaggerate with your mouth and lips "one," but do not say it aloud. Then, say "two" aloud, exaggerate with your mouth and lips "three," and then say "four" aloud. Repeat this sequence several times up to 10 or 20.

Next, have children put their hands in front of them. Without saying the number, have them put up one finger. Say "two" as you put out the second finger. Silently, put up a third finger. As you put out the fourth finger, say "four" aloud. Repeat up to 10. You may want to do this activity several times.

Skip Counting *(cont.)*

HOW *(cont.)*

A fun exercise is to have the children count one another. Point to the first child and silently mouth "one." The next child in the circle or line says "two" aloud. The third child only mouths "three." The fourth child says "four" aloud. Continue until every child has been counted.

Have children sit in different places or switch places in line several times. They will be surprised and enjoy finding out whether they are an unspoken or spoken number each time.

This activity should be varied by alternating which number is skipped—the first or the second. For example, sometimes the skipped or silent number is *one*, so the sequence spoken aloud is 2, 4, 6, 8, etc. Other times, the skipped or silent number is *two*, so the sequence is 1, 3, 5, 7, 9, etc.

One can also incorporate physical activity by having children jump up or clap on the number skipped.

As children become more familiar with this activity, you may even start at different points. For example, you might say, "Let's start at 22 and skip count by twos. Let's say every other number."

HANDS-ON PRACTICE

Make copies of the Skip Counting Practice pages (pages 129–132). After children "skip color" the numbered sections, the colored numbers can be recited. Teachers can also make use of the number cards provided (pages 179–185). Copy even numbers on one color paper and odd numbers on another. Children can lay the numbers in a line and practice reciting the numbers of first one color, and then the other. A teacher can also have children turn over every other card in the line. Then, children can recite the numbers remaining face-up.

CLASS EXTENSIONS

Provide children with 20 beans or other simple counters. Have them count the beans one by one. Then, have the children divide the beans into groups of two. Have them count the beans again, but this time by twos. If children are unsure of counting by two, they can finger or touch each bean. They can count each bean, whispering or silently mouthing the number for the skipped bean, and then saying every other number aloud.

One can also have children trace their feet. The sheets of paper with the traced feet can be taped to the floor. As the children count the number of feet, the teacher can write the number on each foot. Then, children can hop across the floor, landing on every other foot. As they land on each foot, they should say aloud the number foot on which they have landed. Children can start at the foot with the number one or the number two.

Another activity that deals with feet is one that starts with the children sitting in a circle, with their feet extending into the circle. One child stands in the middle of the circle and starts counting feet. The child touches every foot, but skip counts, saying only every other number aloud.

For advanced classes, these activities can be done with skip counting by threes.

Hello,

Today we practiced *skip counting,* or counting every other number. Skip counting is a form of patterning. We started at *one* and at *two,* and then we counted 1, 3, 5, 7, 9 . . . and 2, 4, 6, 8, 10 . . . . Over the course of the year, we will count to higher levels and also begin our counting at different starting points. For example, we may skip count 20 numbers starting at 18, 33, or 105. This activity helps children gain familiarity with number names and understand number sequence and progression. It helps develop the concept of one-to-one correspondence: that every number, even if not spoken, always refers to a specific amount. Our activities with skip counting also provided practice with the basics of addition and multiplication.

Entertain your child by requesting that he or she skip count aloud to pass time while in a car or waiting for something or someone. For example, if your child is a passenger in a car, have him or her skip count cars, trucks, railroad cars, mailboxes, etc. Though your child counts all that he or she sees, only every other number is said aloud.

When your child is still getting used to the idea of skip counting, you may want to take turns saying the numbers. In other words, you say the number your child is skipping. As he or she becomes more familiar with the concept of skip counting, your child can whisper or clap the skipped number, and then say the next number in a loud voice. At some point, your child will be able to skip count without having to mouth or whisper the skipped number.

Have your child take turns skip counting from the numbers one and two.

Have fun!

Name _____

Skip Counting Practice

Color the first box one color. Skip a box and then color the next box the same color as the first box. Continue skip coloring all the boxes. Color the skipped boxes a different color.

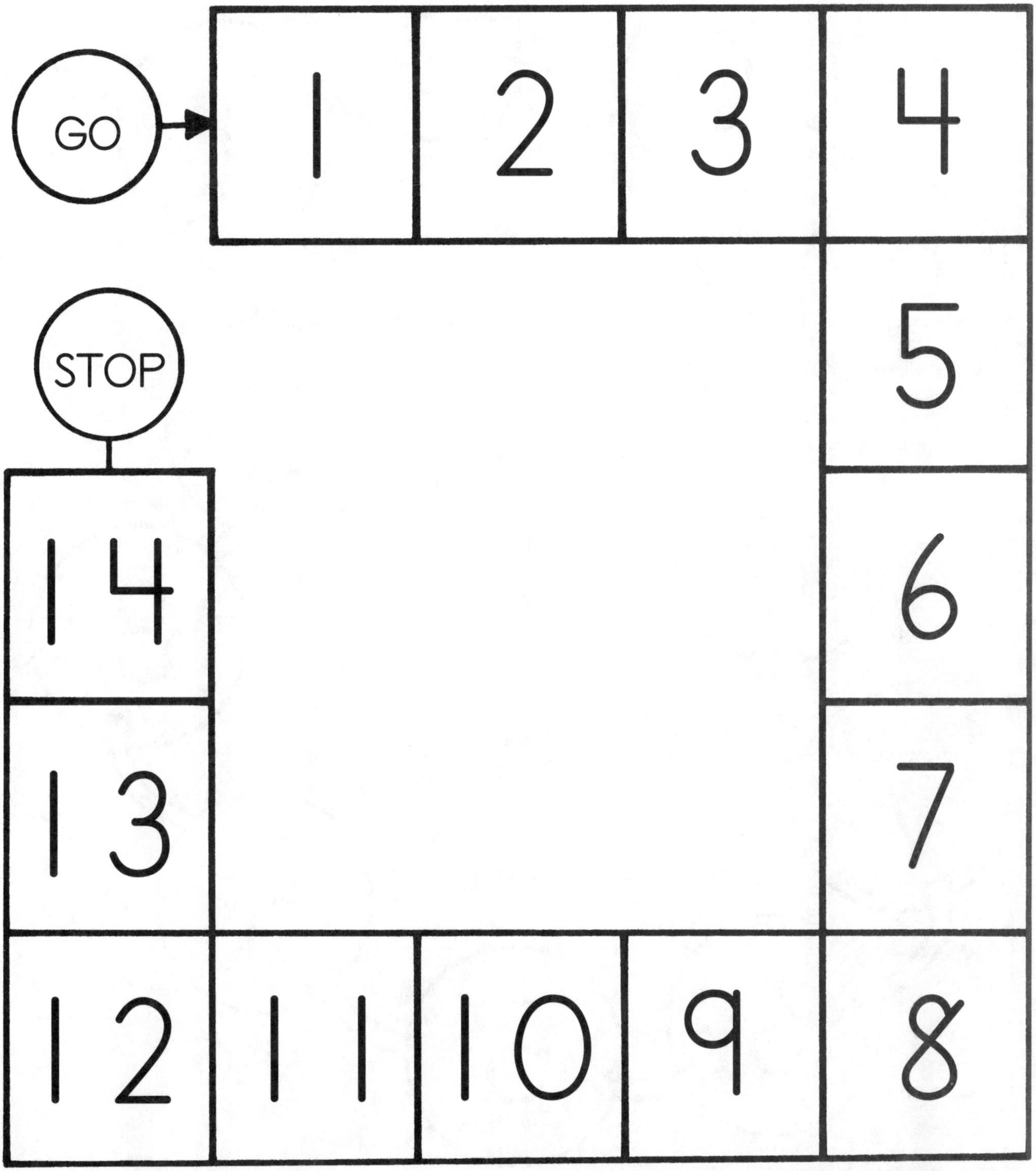

GO →

| 1 | 2 | 3 | 4 |

5

6

7

14			
13			
12	11	10	9	8

STOP

Name _____

Skip Counting Practice *(cont.)*

Start with the number two. Color every other bead.

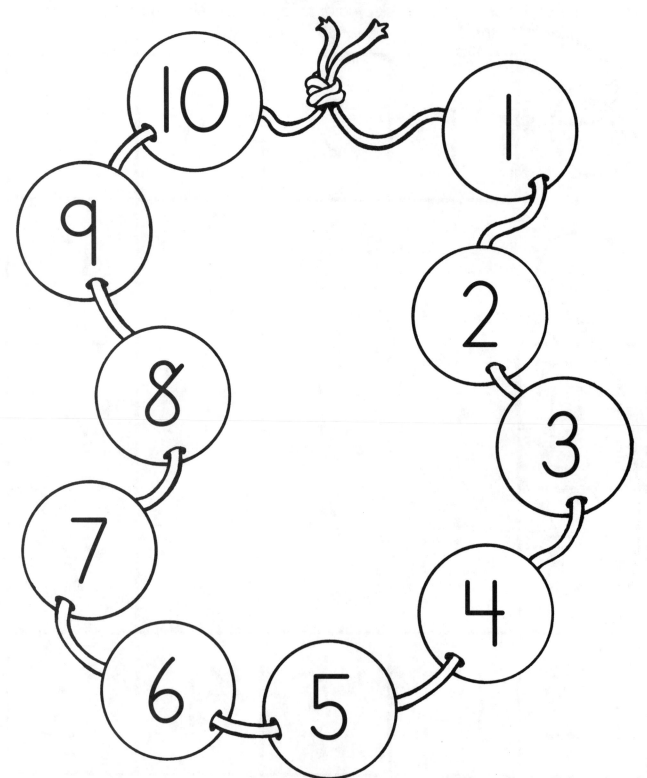

Name _____

Skip Counting Practice *(cont.)*

Start with the number one. Color every other spot.

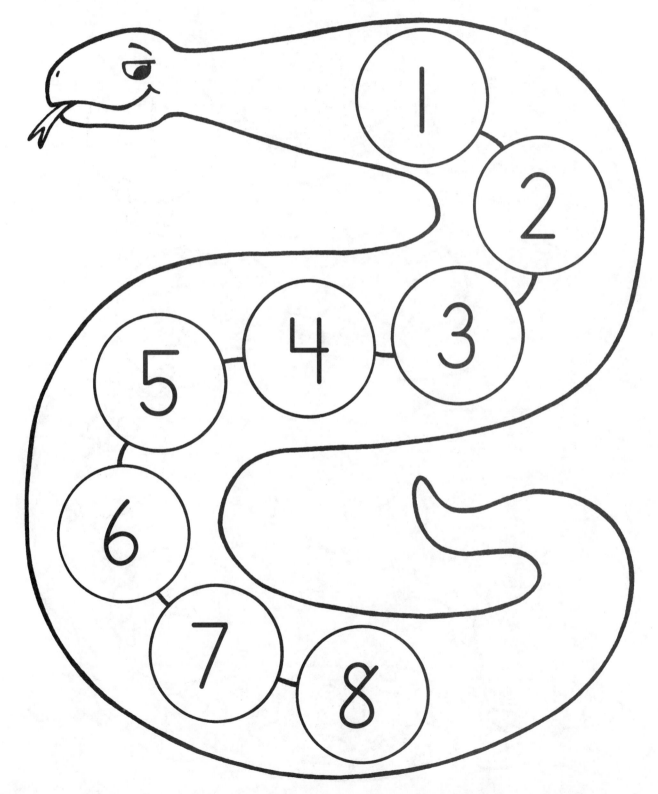

Name _____

Skip Counting Practice *(cont.)*

Start with the number two. Color every other frog.

132 ©*Teacher Created Resources, Inc.*

Counting by 5, 10, and 25

WHAT

Counting in increments, such as by 5, 10, and 25, is an activity that reinforces counting by ones and develops higher math skills. In fact, it is an early introduction to what multiplication entails.

This lesson focuses on number sequence and counting by 5s, 10s, and 25s. It also includes beginning at different starting points while counting in sets of 5, 10, and 25.

Counting by 5, 10, and 25 is presented in one lesson because the procedures and methods are the same for each counting type.

WHY

Counting in increments allows a child to practice number names while strengthening his or her understanding of the number sequence. This particular exercise, of counting in sets of 5, 10, and 25, provides a child with:

- a familiarity with number names
- an understanding of number sequence and progression
- the basics for counting money
- the ability to count starting from various points
- the beginning skills needed for multiplication

HOW

It is recommended that a teacher start with counting by 10s. Once students begin to exhibit mastery, a teacher can begin working on counting by 5s. Counting by 25s should follow. Counting by 10s, 5s, and 25s should not be introduced on the same day.

The first step involves repeating a sequence of numbers and having children join in and repeat the sequence. For example, the first sequence would be 10, 20, 30, etc., up to 100. (A following lesson would introduce the sequence 5, 10, 15, 20, etc., up to 100, while the last lesson would involve repeating 25, 50, 75, 100.)

The sequence should be repeated several times. To add variety, one can request that the sequence be repeated as loudly, quickly, softly, and slowly as one can. As children become more familiar with the numbers, one can even have them shout or whisper every other number.

As proficiency is gained, a teacher will want to modify his or her request by changing the starting points and counting higher. For example, ask the children to start at 40 and go on to 140, counting by 10s; counting by 5s; 50 to 150, counting by 25s, etc.

If a teacher feels that a physical release should be incorporated, he or she can announce ahead of time, "We are going to count from 60 to 160 by tens. When we say the number 100 we are going to jump up (or clap hands, stamp feet, etc.). I wonder who will know exactly when to jump?"

Counting by 5, 10, and 25 *(cont.)*

HOW *(cont.)*

This activity can be coupled with printed numbers as visual aids. A teacher might choose to focus only on the spoken exercise at first and then add visual aids, or he or she might combine them from the beginning. The teacher could point to numbers printed on the board or hold up cards of the numbers as they are spoken.

Once children begin to gain some mastery over counting, practice can occur several times a day as an entertaining time filler. While children are waiting in line or at the beginning or end of activities, a teacher can request for them to count by 1s, then by 10s, 5s, and 25s from varying starting points to varying ending points.

HANDS-ON PRACTICE

Make copies of the number cards (pages 179–185) and have children trace or color them. Keep the 5s, 10s, and 25s separate. Have the children lay out a number set in front of them (all 10's for example). Call out a number and have the children pick out the one named and hold it up.

Children can also mix up their number sets and then place them back in proper order.

Have children turn a 10 into a 15, a 20 into a 25, a 30 into a 35, etc., by first having them lay out the 10 series in order in front of them. Next, have them take a card with the number 5. They should name 10, and then place the 5 over the 0 in the 10 and say 15. They should then say 20 and with the same 5 they used before, put it on the 0 of the 20 and say 25, etc.

CLASS EXTENSIONS

Count out ten piles of ten beans each. (Each child can count out one pile, or perhaps teams of children can count out each pile.) As a class, start counting the beans one by one. At some point, state that this is taking too long and a faster way is needed. Start counting by 10s, pointing to each set of ten as one adds/names another set.

If possible, use real money as 1, 5, 10, and 25 counters. Using real money also gives children experience with the different coin weights.

HOME PAGE

Hello,

Today we practiced counting by **tens**. We started at ten and went up to 100. Over the course of the year, we will count to higher levels and also begin our counting at different starting points. For example, we will count from 130 to 230; 70 to 170; etc.

This activity helps a child gain familiarity with number names and understand number sequence and progression. It will help a child start counting from varying starting points, as well as prepare him or her for counting money. In addition, it provides practice with the roots of multiplication.

Entertain your child by asking him or her to count aloud by tens to pass time while in a car or waiting for something or someone.

Your child will also enjoy counting the number of coins in your wallet. After the number of coins has been counted, separate the coins into piles worth ten cents each. Have your child count by tens to add up the coins' worth.

Have fun!

HOME PAGE

Hello,

Today we practiced counting by **fives**. We started at five and went up to 100. Over the course of the year, we will count to higher levels and also begin our counting at different starting points. For example, we will count from 35 to 135; 55 to 155; etc.

This activity helps a child gain familiarity with number names and understand number sequence and progression. It will help a child start counting from varying starting points, as well as prepare him or her for counting money. In addition, it provides practice with the roots of multiplication.

Entertain your child by asking him or her to count aloud by fives to pass time while in a car or waiting for something or someone.

Your child will also enjoy counting the number of coins in your wallet. After the number of coins has been counted, separate the coins into piles worth five cents each. Have your child count by fives to add up the coins' worth.

Have fun!

HOME PAGE

Hello,

Today we practiced counting by **25s**. We started at 25 and went up to 100. Over the course of the year, we will count to higher levels and also begin our counting at different starting points. For example, we will count from 200 to 300; 525 to 625; etc.

This activity helps a child gain familiarity with number names and understand number sequence and progression. It will help a child start counting from varying starting points, as well as prepare him or her for counting money. In addition, it provides practice with the roots of multiplication.

Ask your child to count aloud by 25s to pass time while in a car or waiting for something or someone.

Your child will also enjoy counting the number of coins in your wallet. After the number of coins has been counted, separate the coins into piles worth 25 cents each. Have your child count by 25s to add up the coins' worth.

Have fun!

Ordinal Numbers

WHAT

Ordinal numbers are any numbers used to show where something comes in a series, such as *first*, *second*, and *third*. This activity focuses on introducing ordinal numbers.

WHY

Ordinal numbers are a mathematical concept, but they apply to everyday situations. Children are constantly being told to "First, do this," or "You get to go second," etc. Introducing ordinal numbers in combination with stories and situations where children have to sequence events:

- reinforces the mathematical concept of position and ordinal numbers
- ties mathematical concepts to day-to-day activities
- reinforces number sense
- provides practice sequencing (first vs. second)
- develops reasoning skills

HOW

Before starting this lesson, a teacher may want to make copies of the number cards (pages 179–180) to use as visual aids, as well as some of the Ordinal Numbers Practice pages (pages 142–147). The practice pages can be used for both the lesson and as a hands-on activity. Having children repeat, by themselves, what was done as a group in class will reinforce the lesson.

Start off this lesson by calling out the name of one child and having that child stand up. Then, call out the name of another child and have that child stand up. Ask the class, "Who stood up first?" If children need direction, lead them to the answer by saying, "Who stood up first? The person who stood up first was not second. He or she is wearing . . . ." Hand the child who stood up first the card with 1 printed on it.

Now, ask the class, "Who stood up second?" Hand the child the card with 2 printed on it. Ask another child to stand up, and ask, "Who stood up third?" Again, hand the child a card, this time with 3 printed on it. Continue until you have 10 children (or whatever number is appropriate for your class) standing.

Arrange the children so that they are actually standing in a line or circle in the sequence of the cards they hold. Pointing to each corresponding child, repeat the words, "First, second, third, fourth," etc. Have each child hold up the number card as he or she is pointed to and as the ordinal word is pronounced. A teacher may want the class to repeat the ordinal words several times.

After the children have reseated themselves and the number cards have been collected, explain that words like *first, second,* and *third* are very important because they help us know in which order things go. Provide children with a set of examples where they have to determine which came first. For example,

"When I wake up in the morning, do I eat breakfast first, or do I get out of bed first? What do I do second, third, fourth?"

Ordinal Numbers *(cont.)*

HOW *(cont.)*

"When I come to school, what do I do first? Do I put my things in my cubby, or do I eat a snack? What do I do second, third, fourth?"

"When I get dressed, what do I do first? Do I put on my shoes, or do I put on my socks? What do I do second, third, fourth?"

"When I get ready for bed, do I take a bath first, brush my teeth, or ride my bike? What do I do first, second, third?"

"When I cook something, do I first mix the ingredients together, or do I first put everything in the oven?"

By this time, many children will need a physical release. Give them orders using ordinal words. Try the following sequence.

- First, stand up.

- Second, jump up and down.

- Third, stretch your arms up to the sky.

- Fourth, touch your toes.

- Fifth, stand on your tip-toes, etc.

It is up to a teacher whether or not he or she wants to spend some time on the phrase *ordinal numbers*. If he or she does, the word *ordinal* should be printed on a piece of paper. Children should repeat the word *ordinal* about 25 times. The repetitions can be divided up into sets of five, with different sets being spoken quickly, slowly, loudly, softly, and in silly voices. Depending on what other activities a teacher has engaged in, children can identify vowels, count the number of syllables and letters, identify beginning and ending letters and sounds, and write the word in the air.

Finally, tell children that they have gotten so good with words like *first, second,* and *third* that now they are going to be First, Second, and Third Detectives. If a teacher has spent time introducing the word *ordinal*, children should be called Ordinal Number Detectives. Hold up or pin copies of the pictures (pages 142–147) on the board. (**Note:** If possible, enlarge the pictures provided.) Ask children to place them in sequential order. (Which happened first, second, third, and fourth, or last?)

A teacher may choose to continue to engage in activities that highlight ordinal numbers at this time or throughout the year. For example, have children:

- pick out the first, second, third, etc., letter of the alphabet
- pick out the first, second, third, etc., letter of their names
- when mentioning the days of the school week, say, "Today is Tuesday, the second day of our school week."
- when mentioning the date, say, "Today is May 24, 2005. It is the 24th day of May."

Ordinal Numbers *(cont.)*

HANDS-ON PRACTICE

Make copies of Ordinal Numbers Practice pages (pages 142–147) for each child. Children can color, cut out, and then paste the cards onto another sheet of paper in the correct order. If children are able, have them print the corresponding number under each picture.

CLASS EXTENSION

Make a copy of the worksheet below for each child. Ask children to think about all the things they have done during the year. Have them come up with ten activities and write them on a piece of scratch paper. Next, have them order these activities in sequence, so that they are marked first, second, third, etc. Rewrite the activites in order.

Ten Things I Have Done This Year

I _____ .

I _____ .

I _____ .

I _____ .

I _____ .

I _____ .

I _____ .

I _____ .

I _____ .

I _____ .

HOME PAGE

Hello,

Today we talked about words that show where something comes in a series, such as *first, second,* and *third.* We engaged in activities where children had to decide what came first, second, and third in different situations so that mathematical concepts could be tied to day-to-day activities.

Practice with these types of words reinforces number sense. It also develops reasoning skills, as a child determines what must happen before something else.

Engage your child in First, Second, and Third Detective games where he or she has to find the word that fits. For example, ask your child the following:

- Are you first, second, third, etc., born?

- As you get into the car, what did you do first? Do you open the door, buckle your seatbelt, or close the door?

- If you are number ten in line, are you tenth or eleventh?

- Is our home the first, second, etc., house or apartment on the street?

- Which came first, second, and third: puddles of water on the ground, the sun being covered by dark clouds, or rain?

Have fun!

Ordinal Numbers Practice

Cut out and color the picture cards. Place the pictures in the order of what happened **first**, **second**, **third**, and **fourth** or last.

Ordinal Numbers Practice *(cont.)*

Cut out and color the picture cards. Place the pictures in the order of what happened **first, second, third,** and **fourth** or last.

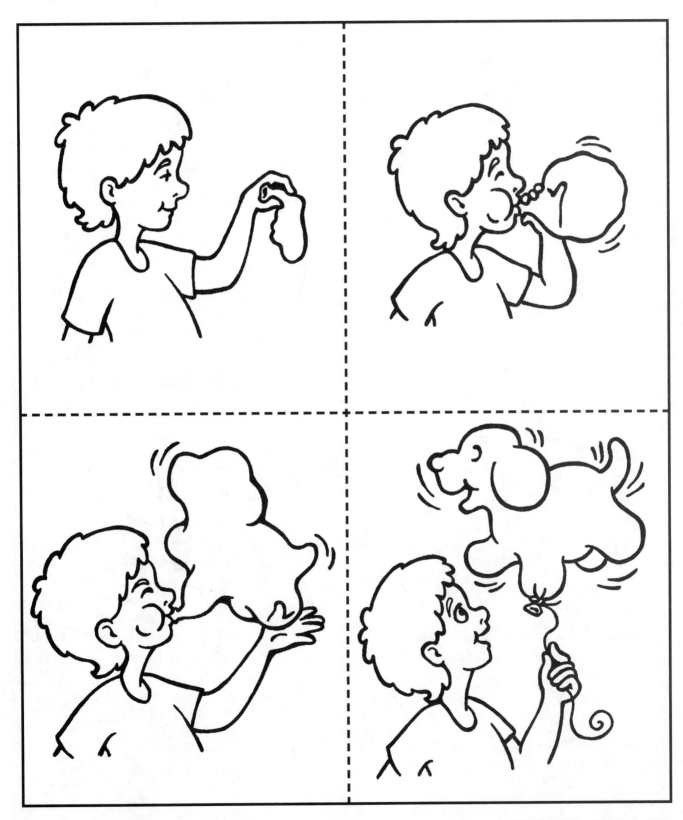

Ordinal Numbers Practice *(cont.)*

Cut out and color the picture cards. Place the pictures in the order of what happened **first, second, third,** and **fourth** or last.

Ordinal Numbers Practice *(cont.)*

Cut out and color the picture cards. Place the pictures in the order of what happened **first, second, third,** and **fourth** or last.

Ordinal Numbers Practice *(cont.)*

Cut out and color the picture cards. Place the pictures in the order of what happened **first**, **second**, **third**, and **fourth** or last.

Ordinal Numbers Practice *(cont.)*

Cut out and color the picture cards. Place the pictures in the order of what happened **first, second, third,** and **fourth** or last.

Evens and Odds

WHAT

Every whole number is either even or odd. *Odd* numbers end in 1, 3, 5, 7, and 9. *Even* numbers end in 0, 2, 4, 6, and 8. This activity focuses on separating numbers into evens and odds.

WHY

It is not expected that children of preschool age understand the mathematical difference between even and odd numbers. An early introduction to even and odd numbers can provide children:

- practice with identification of the numbers 0, 1, 2, 3, 4, 5, 6, 7, 8, and 9
- practice focusing on a specific detail—an "end" number—both auditory and visual
- practice with sorting and classification
- familiarity with number names (*hundreds, thousands, millions*, etc.)

HOW

Recite the numbers 0–9 while pointing to or holding up corresponding printed cards. Describe how just as we can separate children into groups of boys and girls, hats by color, and animals by size, we can separate numbers into evens and odds. All numbers, no matter what color the letter is, or how big or small, are even or odd. All even numbers end in 0, 2, 4, 6, and 8. All odd numbers end in 1, 3, 5, 7, and 9. Have the children recite this rhyme several times:

> 0, 2, 4, 6, and 8. Who do we appreciate?
>
> Even numbers, even numbers, yay!
>
> 1, 3, 5, 7, and 9. What do we find really fine?
>
> Odd numbers, odd numbers, yay!

Set up a question-and-answer dialogue where one asks students to identify numbers as even or odd. One can do this using both or either the visual and auditory modes. If a teacher wants visual reinforcement, he or she may choose to place the numbers 0–9 in two separate groups, explaining that one group is odd and that the other is even. A sample dialogue may proceed as follows:

"Three, is it even or odd?"

"Thirty-three, is it even or odd?"

3

"This is too easy! I'm going to give you a really big number. 333! Is it even or odd?"

3

"What about this enormous number—5,493. Is it even or odd?"

3

Evens and Odds *(cont.)*

HOW *(cont.)*

Continue with numbers in the 10,000's, 100,000's, and millions.

Note: If numbers are only being spoken and not presented with a visual prompt, one must take care not to recite a number that ends with a zero (100, 500, 1,000, 10,000, etc.) or a teen number (11, 12, 13, 14, etc.), for the child is unable to hear an ending digit. This lesson focuses on the importance of the last digit and differentiating numbers. Knowing the difference between 1,000's and 10,000's at this point is not important. What is important is that the names of the numbers are being introduced, as well as the concept that there is a great number of numbers that, despite their size, can be sorted.

If there is a visual prompt, any number can be used.

HANDS-ON PRACTICE

After copying number sets, from 1–10 (pages 179–180), for each student, have students color or trace the number cards. Ask them to separate them into evens and odds. Have the children make up bigger numbers with their cards, lining them up, perhaps three in a row. Ask them whether the new number is even or odd.

Provide a copy for each student of the Evens and Odds Practice pages (pages 151–154). Direct the children to circle the odd or even numbers.

CLASS EXTENSIONS

Have children decide if the current date is even or odd. Ask them what yesterday's date and tomorrow's date will be—even or odd?

Have children visualize a particular object in their heads—a car, for example. Ask them questions about its even and odd properties.

"Think about the wheels. Are there an even or odd number of wheels?"

"Is there an odd or even number of steering wheels?"

"Is there an odd or even number of doors?"

One can also ask children about their own even and odd properties.

"You have two legs. Do you have an even number of legs or an odd number of legs?"

"Do you have an odd number of noses or an even number?"

"Do you have an even or odd number of eyes?"

"Are you an odd or an even age? What will you be next year?"

HOME PAGE

Hello,

Today we sorted numbers into evens or odds. Odd numbers end in 1, 3, 5, 7, and 9. Even numbers end in 0, 2, 4, 6, and 8.

It is not expected that children of preschool age understand the mathematical difference between even and odd numbers, but an early introduction of even and odd numbers can help children practice with identification of the numbers 0–9, focusing on a specific detail (the end number), and find familiarity with number names like *hundreds* and *thousands*.

Call out numbers while pushing your child on a swing, driving in the car, or waiting in lines and then ask, "Even or odd?" For example, Call out:

"Two million and one! Is it even or odd?"

"Three million and one! Is it even or odd?"

"Four million and one! Is it even or odd?"

"Forty-four million and one! Is it even or odd?"

Point out numbers on food boxes or signs and ask, "Even or odd?"

Ask questions such as these:

"Is there an odd number of people or an even number of people in this car?"

"There are five plates on the table. Is there an even or an odd number of plates?"

"You are four-years-old. Are you even or odd?"

"Your name has five letters in it. Is that an even or odd number of letters?"

"We live at 2508 Jackson Street. Is our address even or odd?"

"All the numbers on one side of the street are even. All the numbers on the other side of the street are odd. What side are we on?"

Have fun!

Name _____

Evens and Odds Practice

Circle the plates with an **odd** number of cookies.

Odd numbers end in 1, 3, 5, 7, and 9.

Name _____

Evens and Odds Practice *(cont.)*

Circle the fish bowls with an **even** number of fish.

Even numbers end in 0, 2, 4, 6, and 8.

152 ©*Teacher Created Resources, Inc.*

Name _____

Evens and Odds Practice *(cont.)*

Circle the **even** numbers in each row. Even numbers end in 0, 2, 4, 6, and 8.

7	22	8	18	108	55
10	4	1	36	13	2

Evens and Odds Practice *(cont.)*

Circle the **odd** numbers in each row. Odd numbers end in 1, 3, 5, 7, and 9.

9	99	2	44	1	103
6	7	35	21	8	91

154

Big, Bigger, Biggest

WHAT

We assess and evaluate everything around us everyday. Making decisions as to what is *big*, what is *bigger*, and what is *biggest* is one of the most basic types of evaluations we perform. This lesson focuses on making decisions as to what is big, what is bigger, and what is biggest.

WHY

Children need practice evaluating information they are given. They need practice sorting through the information and coming to a decision about it. Preschool children are still deciding exactly what "big" means. Both adults and school buses are described as big, so which one is really big? Engaging children in activities where they have to make big/bigger/biggest decisions allows a child to:

- apply reasoning skills
- practice judging the size of one object relative to another object
- practice judging an amount relative to another quantity

HOW

A teacher may want to prepare some visual prompts ahead of time. The prompts do not need to be fancy. They should be three things from the same category (as in balls, books, cups, plates, pieces of paper, shoes, etc.) and in three distinctive sizes so that it is very clear which one is bigger and which one is biggest.

Engage children in a discussion where you ask them what is "big." Most children will explain by naming something that is big. When appropriate, you might want to say something like, "But would it be big if you were an enormous elephant? What if you were a big dinosaur?"

Hold up a set of your first visual prompts, three socks for example. Say to children, "If we call this one big (the smallest sock), then what is this one?" If the children do not come up with the word *bigger* by themselves, direct them to it by asking, "If we say this one is big (lift up the first sock), can we say this one is bigger?"

Finally, hold up the third and last sock and say, "Okay, we have big and bigger, so what is this?" If the children do not come up with the word *biggest* on their own, direct them to it by asking, "If we say this one is big (first sock), and this one is bigger (second sock), can we say that this one is the biggest?"

Before bringing up your other visual prompts, have children repeat several times the words *big, bigger,* and *biggest.* If desired, have the children repeat the words while they engage in different activities such as jumping up, speaking loudly, speaking softly, and with their eyes closed.

After children are comfortable with the words *big, bigger,* and *biggest*, bring out the remainder of your visual prompts and have children name them as big, bigger, or biggest.

A teacher will want to engage children in some physical activities as well as activities where a child is required to create a visual picture and make a decision based on that. Depending on what the class needs, a teacher can combine these two types of activities or perform them separately.

Big, Bigger, Biggest *(cont.)*

HOW *(cont.)*

For physical activities, a teacher may have children speak in a big, then bigger, then biggest voice, as well as jump, stretch, take a step, clap, pound on the floor, stamp their feet, etc.

Some sample questions that do not involve physical activities might be the following:

"I have a doughnut. I just divided it into three pieces. Would you like the big, bigger, or biggest piece?"

"We are going on a walk. There are three trails we can take. Do you want to go on the big one-mile walk, the bigger two-mile walk, or the biggest three-mile walk?"

"A long time ago there were dinosaurs. One dinosaur was the size of this chair. One dinosaur was as big as a bus. One dinosaur was as big as a car. Which dinosaur was the biggest? Which dinosaur was just big? Which dinosaur was bigger?"

A teacher or a child can also name something. The class as a whole or one other child then needs to name something bigger than what is named. The class as a whole or a third child needs to come up with something that is biggest. This particular activity can be done throughout the year. It is a great time-filler when there are just a few minutes left.

HANDS-ON PRACTICE

Make copies of the cards (pages 158–160). Have children color them and then paste them on a piece of paper in the order of big, bigger, and biggest.

One can also have children make three groups of blocks, clay, or crackers into big, bigger, and biggest piles.

A teacher may also want to use the cards from the small/smaller/smallest lesson (pages 165–166), this time having children paste them in the opposite order.

CLASS EXTENSION

Bring up the fact that sometimes it is very hard to figure out what is big, bigger, and biggest. Put out three cups. Using beans or something else as small, have the class say aloud "one," and then put one bean in every cup. Continue this up to 10. At this point, move one cup aside. Have the class count "11, 12," putting a bean in each cup as the number is recited. Move aside a second cup so that there is only one left. As the children say "13, 14," put in two more beans. The result should be that the three cups of beans are filled with three close, but different, amounts of beans. One cup will have 10 beans, another 12, and the last, 14.

HOME PAGE

Hello,

Today we practiced making decisions about what is *big, bigger,* and *biggest*. We looked at the same item in different sizes, but we also practiced making big, bigger, and biggest steps and jumps.

This activity allows a child to apply reasoning skills. He or she also practices judging size and amount relative to other objects and quantities.

Engage your child with questions about what is big, bigger, and biggest.

1. Say the name of an item, or have your child say its name. The next person has to come up with something bigger and biggest.

2. Ask your child to clap, stomp, jump, stretch, or take a step. The first time is big, the second is bigger, the third is biggest.

3. List three things and have your child put them in the order of big, bigger, biggest. (Family members and animals are always popular for this type of question.)

4. Ask your child to find the biggest _____. (This one is great for filling time while waiting or driving.)

Have fun!

Big, Bigger, Biggest Practice

Cut out and color the pictures. Arrange them in order from **big**, **bigger**, and **biggest**. Paste the pictures in order on another page.

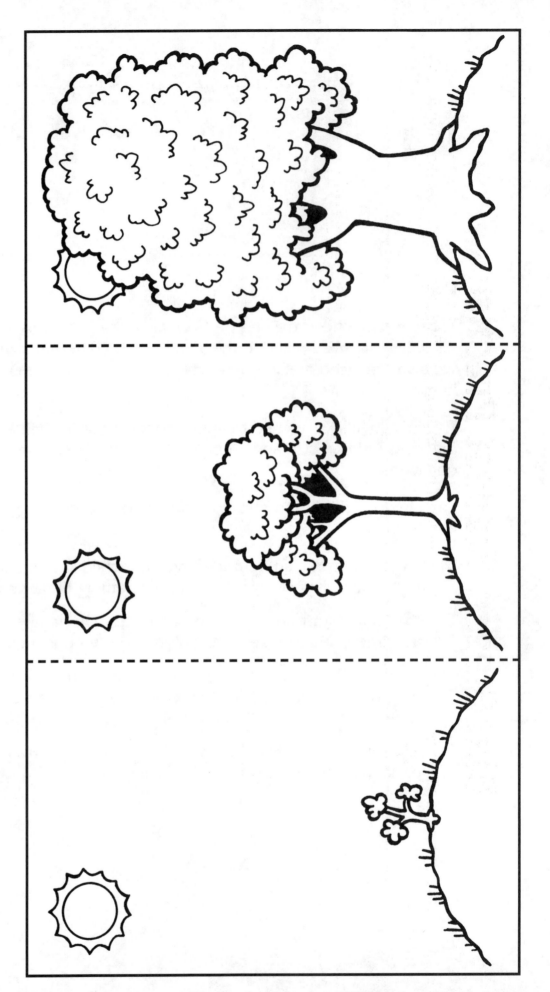

Big, Bigger, Biggest Practice *(cont.)*

Cut out and color the pictures. Arrange them in order from **big**, **bigger**, and **biggest**. Paste the pictures in order on another page.

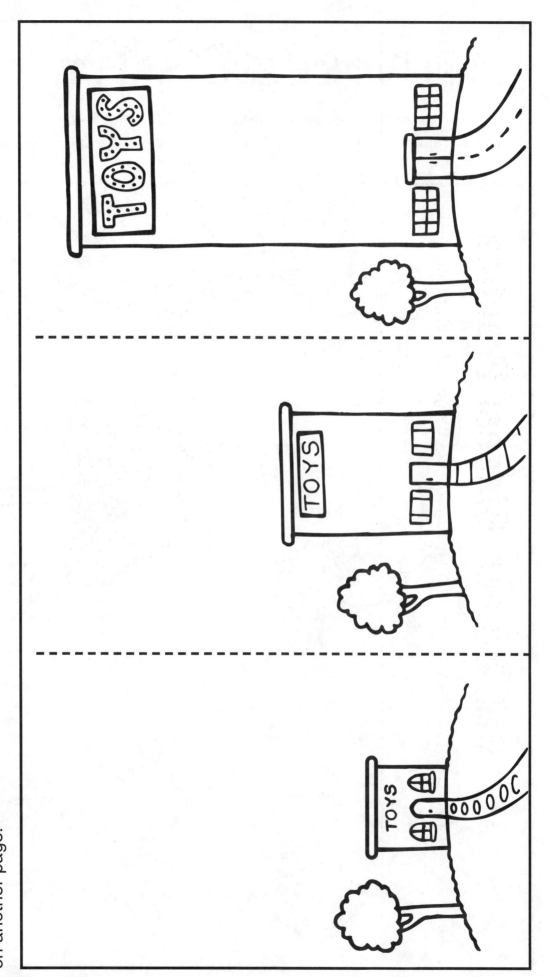

Big, Bigger, Biggest Practice *(cont.)*

Cut out and color the pictures. Arrange them in order from **big, bigger,** and **biggest.** Paste the pictures in order on another page.

Small, Smaller, Smallest

WHAT

We assess and evaluate everyday. Making decisions as to what is *small*, what is *smaller*, and what is *smallest* is one of the most basic types of evaluations we perform. This lesson focuses on making decisions as to what is small, what is smaller, and what is smallest.

WHY

Children need practice evaluating information they are given. They need practice sorting through the information and coming to a decision about it. Preschool children are still deciding exactly what *small* means. Children hear themselves referred to as small, but then so are ants! So what is truly small? Engaging children in activities where they have to make *small/smaller/smallest* decisions allows them to:

- apply reasoning skills
- practice judging the size of one object relative to another object
- practice judging an amount relative to another quantity
- contrast small/smaller/smallest relationships to big/bigger/biggest relationships

HOW

A teacher may want to prepare some visual props ahead of time. The props do not need to be fancy. They should be three things from the same category (as in balls, books, cups, plates, pieces of paper, shoes, etc.) and in three distinctive sizes so that it is very clear which one is small and which one is smallest.

If a teacher has recently engaged in the big/bigger/biggest lesson, he or she may want to use some of the same props. This allows children to understand the relativity of position. Something that was biggest, when compared for smallness against other things, is now small.

Engage children in a discussion where you ask them what *small* means. Most children will explain by naming something that is physically small. When appropriate, you might want to say something like, "But would it be small if you were a spider? How about if you were an elephant?"

Hold up a set of your first visual prompts, three plates for example. Say to children, "If we call this one small (hold up a normal dinner-sized paper plate), then what is this one (hold up a small paper plate)?" If children do not come up with the word *smaller* by themselves, direct them to it by asking, "If we say this one is small (lift up the dinner plate), can we say this one is smaller (lift up the smaller plate)?"

Finally, hold up the third plate, from a doll's tea set perhaps. Say, "Okay, we have small and smaller, so what is this?" If the children do not come up with the word *smallest* on their own, direct them to it by asking, "If we say this one is small (first plate), and this one is smaller (second plate), can we say that this one is the smallest?"

Small, Smaller, Smallest *(cont.)*

HOW *(cont.)*

Before showing your other visual prompts, have children repeat several times the words *small, smaller,* and *smallest*. If desired, have the children repeat the words while they engage in different activities such as jumping up, speaking loudly, speaking softly, and with their eyes closed.

After children are comfortable with the words *small, smaller,* and *smallest*, bring out the remainder of your visual prompts and have children name them as small, smaller, or smallest.

A teacher will want to engage children in some physical activities, as well as activities where a child is required to create a visual picture and make a decision based on that. Depending on what the class needs, a teacher can combine these two types of activities or perform them separately.

For physical activities, a teacher may have children speak in a small, then smaller, then smallest voice, as well as jump, stretch, take a step, clap, pound on the floor, stamp their feet, etc.

Some sample questions that do not involve physical activities might be the same ones used for the big, bigger, and biggest questions interchanged with the words *small, smaller,* and *smallest*, as well as these new ones.

"I have a cake. I just cut it into three pieces. Would you like the small, smaller, or smallest piece?"

"There are three swinging bridges across a high, high canyon. Would you feel more comfortable walking across the small bridge, the smaller bridge, or the smallest bridge?" (A teacher might want to spread his or her hands apart with each description so that the children realize he or she is talking about width.)

"I just found a bug in my shoe! Would you prefer to find a small bug, a smaller bug, or the smallest bug in your shoe?"

"There are three cats. One of them is just a baby. I can carry it with one hand. The other one is all grown up. I can only lift it if I use two hands. The third one is half-grown. Which cat is the smallest? Which cat is just small? Which cat is smaller?"

A teacher or a child can also name something. The class as a whole or one other child then needs to name something smaller than what was named. The class, as a whole, or a third child needs to come up with something that is smallest. This particular activity can be done throughout the year. It is a great time-filler when there are just a few minutes. It's great fun to contrast it right away with what is big, bigger, and biggest!

Small, Smaller, Smallest *(cont.)*

HANDS-ON PRACTICE

Make copies of the cards (pages 165–166). Have children color them and then paste them on a sheet of paper in the order of small, smaller, and smallest. A teacher may also want to reuse the cards from the big/bigger/biggest lesson (pages 158–160), this time having children paste them in the opposite order.

One can also have children make three groups of blocks, clay, or crackers into small, smaller, and smallest piles.

To practice fine-motor skills, a teacher may have children draw a line or a circle on a piece of paper. Next, have them draw a smaller line right below the first line or a smaller circle inside the circle they just drew. Finally, have children draw an even smaller line underneath the other two or a smaller circle inside the other circles.

CLASS EXTENSIONS

Give children a page from the newspaper. Have them find three different sizes of words. Then, have the children describe the words as small, smaller, and smallest (and if you want, big, bigger, and biggest).

One can also use the same counting activities used in the big/bigger/biggest class extension lesson. Instead of pointing out what is big/bigger/biggest, children instead point out what is small/smaller/smallest.

HOME PAGE

Hello,

Today we practiced making decisions about what is *small, smaller,* and *smallest.* We looked at the same item in different sizes, but we also practiced making small, smaller, and smaller steps and jumps.

This activity allows a child to apply reasoning skills. Children also practice judging size and amount relative to other objects and quantities.

Engage your child with questions about what is small, smaller, and smallest.

1. Say the name of an item, or have your child say its name. The next person has to come up with something smaller and smallest.

2. Ask your child to clap, stomp, jump, stretch, or take a step. The first time is small, the second time is smaller, the third time is the smallest.

3. List three things and have the child put them in the order of small, smaller, smallest. (Family members and animals are always popular for this type of question.)

4. Ask your child to find the smallest _____. (This one is great for filling time while waiting or driving.)

If you want, take your small lists and items and have children redo them in the order of big, bigger, biggest.

Have fun!

Small, Smaller, Smallest Practice

Cut out and color the pictures. Arrange them in order from **small, smaller,** and **smallest.** Paste the pictures in order on another page.

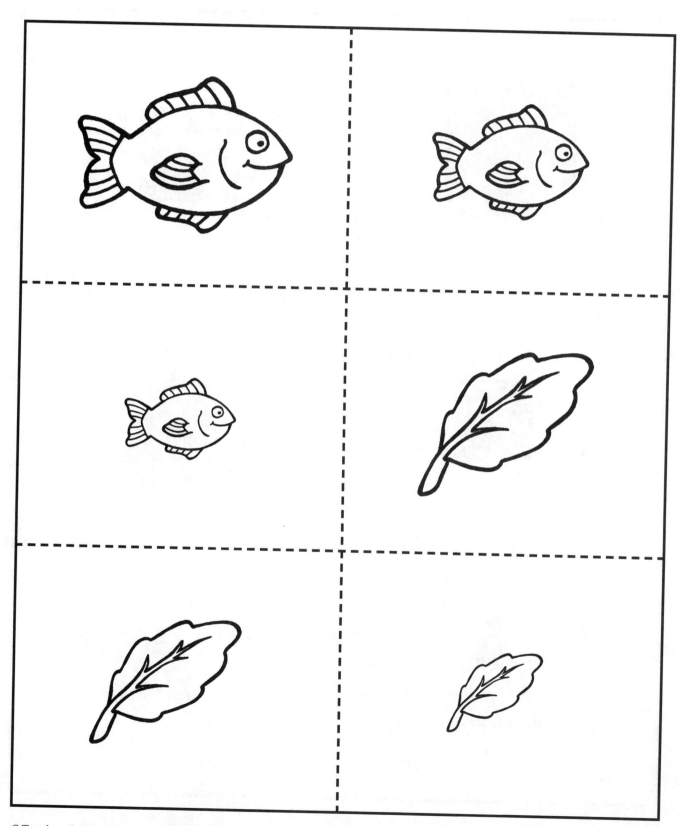

Small, Smaller, Smallest Practice *(cont.)*

Cut out and color the pictures. Arrange them in order from **small, smaller,** to **smallest.** Paste the pictures in order on another page.

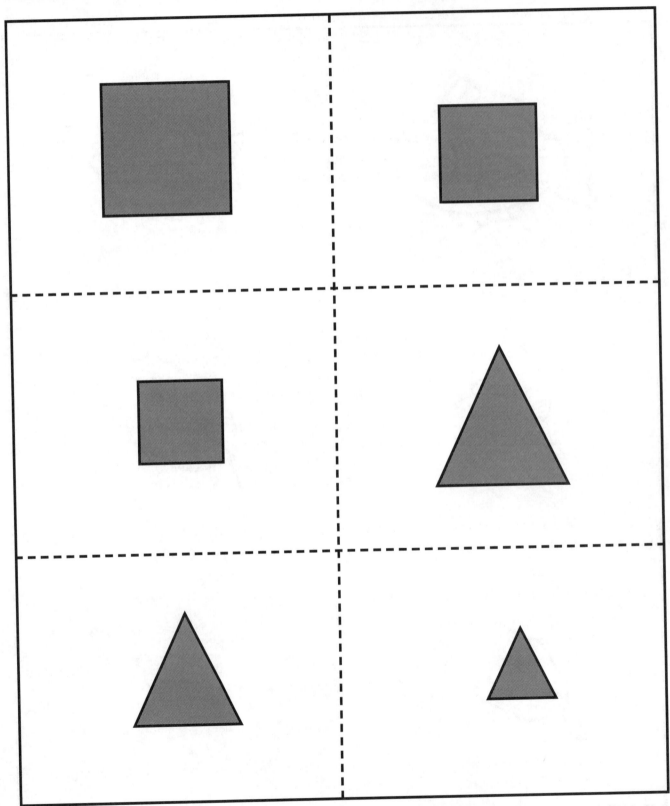

Greater Than/Less Than

WHAT

Greater than/less than decisions are a form of comparison. We evaluate two sides and make a decision as to which is greater. It requires making a judgment. This lesson focuses on making *greater than/less than* decisions.

WHY

Children will be required to work with the terms *greater than* and *less than* in school, most commonly in math when they are comparing numbers. Greater than/*less than* comparisons are not limited to school. We evaluate two sides and make a decision as to which is *greater than* or *less than* in everyday activities. Engaging children in *greater than/less than* activities help them:

- develop reasoning skills
- practice judging size and amount relative to another object and quantity
- learn terms and concepts they will need to apply later on in school
- become familiar with numbers

HOW

Engage children with a visual demonstration. Break a cookie or tear a piece of bread or paper (or anything else available that can be divided easily) into two uneven bits. Ask children which one is bigger and which one is smaller. Explain that you will be practicing describing the two bits in a new way. You will be saying one is *greater than* or *less than* the other.

Have children practice saying the phrase *greater than* by having them repeat it several times. Have them make big physical movements as they repeat the words so they get physical reinforcement that the *greater than* is the bigger one. One might have the children say the words in a big voice, *greater than* a small voice; jump up really high, *greater than* a small jump; or clap their hands really hard, *greater than* a small clap.

Repeat this with the phrase *less than*. Have children say the words while speaking in a very soft voice, *less than* a great voice; making tiny jumps, *less than* great jumps; or clapping very softly, *less than* great claps.

Continue with other items. A teacher might, for example,

- make two piles of blocks. Ask which pile is *greater than* the other pile, and which pile is *less than* the other pile.
- have children hold up one finger on one hand and five fingers on the other hand. Ask which hand has a greater number of fingers up. Which hand has fewer, or less, fingers up than the other hand?
- divide a clay ball. Ask which lump of clay now is *greater than* the other, and which one has *less than* the other.
- count the number of boys and girls in the class. Decide if there is a greater number of boys or girls. Is the number of girls *less than* the number of boys?

Greater Than/Less Than *(cont.)*

HOW *(cont.)*

- count and decide between chairs and tables; windows and doors; walls and floors; teachers and students; noses and hands; etc.
- make piles on the floor using crayons or felt pens. Ask children which pile is greater than the other, and which pile is less than the other.

Engage children in a question-and-answer session where children have to make these decisions without a hands-on prompt. A teacher might ask, for example, for:

- the number of shoes in this room/number of clocks in this room: Which one is greater? Which one is less?
- the number of flags in this room/number of sinks. Which one is greater? Which one is less?

HANDS-ON PRACTICE

Provide children with tiny crackers or blocks. Instruct them to divide them into two piles. Have children decide which pile has a greater number of blocks or crackers than the other pile. Ask the children which pile has less than the other pile. A teacher may choose to be more structured with this activity and have children put specific numbers in the piles. For example, one cracker in one pile and three in another. Ask the same questions about which pile is greater than the other pile, and which pile is less than the other pile. A teacher may choose to say, "Eat the greater pile!" or, "Eat the pile that has less!" (**Safety Alert:** Check for food allergies before using food items.)

Make copies of the Greater Than/Less Than Practice pages (pages 170–172). On one sheet, have children circle the side that is greater than the other side. On the other sheet, have children circle the side that has less than the other side.

CLASS EXTENSIONS

Make copies of the pictures of the unicycle, bicycle, tricycle, and car (page 170). Have children look at the number of wheels. Have the children order the pictures according to the number of wheels. Then, ask questions about the items. For example,

> "Which has a greater number of wheels—the unicycle or the car?"

> "Does the bicycle have a greater number of wheels than the tricycle?"

> "Which has a greater number of wheels than the bicycle, but less wheels than the car?"

> "Which has less wheels than the car, but a greater number of wheels than the unicycle?"

A great way to reinforce math skills (and introduce algebraic balancing equations) is to add a new step to the activity where children are making two piles of blocks and deciding which pile is greater than the other. Once a decision has been made, a teacher can say, "Put one more block on each pile. Now, which side is greater?" He or she can do this with varying numbers of blocks. The same number of blocks can be added or subtracted from each side. Children will get a hands-on lesson that introduces the concept that "as long as you do the same things to both sides, the answer does not change."

HOME PAGE

Hello,

Today we made greater than/less than comparisons. We made piles, looked at objects, and compared numbers. Each time, we decided which one was greater than the other, and which one was less than the other.

This activity helps to develop reasoning skills and provides practice judging size and amount relative to another object or quantity.

Asking questions about what is greater than and what is less than is a fun way to pass time and occupy a child. For example,

- While shopping, ask your child which can, box, or bag has a greater amount than another item which is next to it on the shelf. Which item has less than the other?

- While driving, ask your child to look at other cars and find one that has a greater number of people and one that has less than the number of people in your own car.

- Decide if the number of boys you see is greater than or less than the number of girls.

- Decide if the number of children you see is greater than or less than the number of adults.

- Decide if the number of birds you see is greater than or less than the number of dogs.

- Decide if the number of houses you see is greater than or less than the number of stores.

Have fun!

Greater Than/Less Than Practice

Cut out and color the pictures. Look at the number of wheels in each picture.
Arrange the pictures in order from the object that has the **least** number of
wheels to the **greatest** number of wheels.

Name _____

Greater Than/Less Than Practice *(cont.)*

Circle the side that is **greater** than the other side.

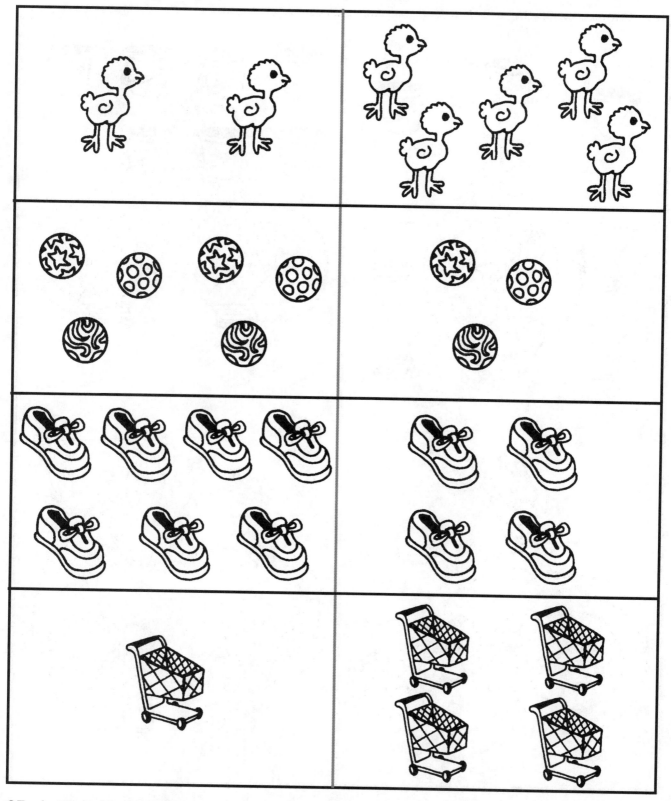

Name _____

Greater Than/Less Than Practice *(cont.)*

Circle the side that is **less** than the other side.

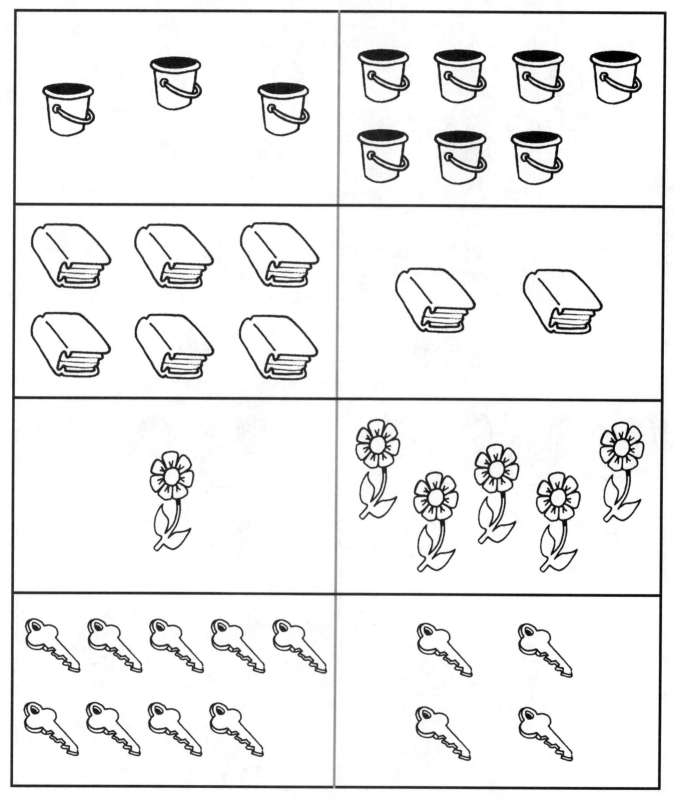

Patterns

WHAT

Something with a *pattern* copies a model and repeats itself. Wallpaper and cloth often have a repeating design or a distinctive pattern. Patterns can be found in mathematics, as well. A figure can be turned over and over in a particular direction, or a number in a series can be determined by what happened to the number in front of it. This lesson focuses on identifying patterns.

WHY

Patterns are basic to much of what we expect children to learn. For example, counting by ones, fives, tens, and other multiples is a pattern. We add a certain number to the one before, creating a series. Patterns can also be seen in everyday occurrences, as on printed cloth, silverware, or tableware. Bringing early attention to patterns helps a child to look at the world with an awareness that there might be similarities and patterns between pieces. This awareness, in turn, develops a child's:

- visual discrimination skills
- understanding of cause and effect (what happened before might determine what happens next)
- reasoning skills (what makes the pattern)
- background for higher mathematical concepts in addition and algebra, as well as geometry

HOW

Before the lesson, a teacher might want to make copies of some of the Patterns Practice pages (pages 176–178) for visual props, or bring in everyday patterned objects such as pieces of silverware, wallpaper, cloth, paper cups, napkins, plates, or other similar items stamped with a pattern. In addition, a teacher might want to write on the board or on strips of paper simple patterned sequences such as:

- A, C, E, G, etc. (every other letter)
- 1, 3, 5, 7, etc. (every other number—this pattern can be started from various starting points)
- 100, 200, 300, 400, etc. (can be done in increments of 2, 5, 10, etc.)
- A, 1, B, 2, C, 3, etc. (letter of alphabet followed by its ordinal position in the alphabet)
- pictures of fruit creating a pattern such as apple, apple, orange, apple, apple, orange, etc.
- square and rectangular blocks arranged in a pattern

Begin the lesson by stating that today the class will be working on something called *patterns*. Explain that a *pattern* is a way of doing things where something is repeated over and over. Immediately start by clapping your hands two times, pausing, and continuing the pattern. Ask the children to begin to clap with you. This was a listening pattern that went two claps, pause, two claps. Continue with several other listening patterns that the children have to figure out. These can be clapped, stamped, or snapped.

Next, tell children that some patterns are looking patterns. They have to look at something and figure out what is being repeated. Have every other child stand up. Point to each child and say the pattern, "Up, down, up, down." Repeat this, with every other child putting his or her hands on top of his or her head, one foot in the circle, etc.

Patterns *(cont.)*

HOW *(cont.)*

Once the children grasp the concept, start the pattern with different children in the circle and see if the rest can finish it. For example, have one child put a hand on his or her foot. Have the next child put a hand on his or her stomach. Ask the third child what he or she thinks the next step in the pattern will be (hand on foot). Continue on around the circle. One might challenge the children further, depending on the circle size and how the class is doing by having every third child do something different. For example, two children put their hands on their heads, but the third child puts his or her hand on the floor.

At this point, the children probably need settling down. Tell them that "looking" patterns aren't always big. Sometimes they are small. Bring out the items such as silverware or paper cups and ask them to describe the pattern that can be found on each of them. Continue with wallpaper, material, etc.

Finally, tell the children that they are so good at identifying patterns that it is time to get to the hard stuff—number and/or written patterns. Hold up one of the sequences you printed and ask the children what the pattern is. If, for example, you put up a sequence of a box, circle, box, circle, you would ask the children what came next. You would draw in the correct response once it is mentioned. Depending on the level of the class, you would continue with different sequences until the children have had enough practice.

This type of exercise can be done throughout the year. The mathematical ones are often the most difficult, but as children become familiar with the task in front of them, they will find it easier and easier. Many of the sequences can be used to reinforce or introduce other lessons. For example, number sequences that go up reinforce or introduce the lesson counting by tens. After patterns are introduced, a teacher might choose to include figuring out a pattern in every circle time or at least once a day during class discussions.

HANDS-ON PRACTICE

Make copies of the Patterns Practice pages (pages 176–178) and have children complete them. A teacher may also have children make up their own patterns. They can do this with pictures, letters, colors, or sound.

Engaging children with paper chain making can also provide hands-on practice with patterns. Children use different colored slips of paper to make up a color pattern and repeat it as they add links. This particular type of activity can also be done with stringing items on a string.

CLASS EXTENSIONS

Have children go on a pattern search where they have to find something with a pattern. They may do this in the classroom or bring something from home.

Teachers can also make standing in line a pattern-setting time. The first and second children are told to do something different from each other. The third child imitates the first child, the fourth child imitates the second, and so on. As children become more advanced, a teacher can make the patterns much more difficult in that instead of being ABAB, they are AABAAB, or ABBABB, or ABCABC, etc.

HOME PAGE

Hello,

Today we talked about patterns. We looked for patterns on everyday things like our clothes, silverware, and paper products. Then, we made our own patterns by clapping, standing, and sitting in different ways. We also looked at the patterns in sequences of objects, numbers, and letters. By figuring out the pattern, we could figure out what came next in the sequence.

This activity helps develops a child's reasoning skills, as well as his or her visual discrimination skills. It helps a child pay attention to what he or she sees.

Involving your child in pattern searches is a great way to entertain him or her. Have your child search for visual patterns in objects around the house. He or she may find a pattern by noting stripes on shirts or how tiles are arranged on the floor or in the shower.

You may have your child listen for auditory patterns, too, by clapping, snapping, or humming a pattern. For example, you can repeat clap, pause, clap; clap, pause, clap. The search is on to figure out what comes next!

Have fun!

Patterns Practice

Name _____

Look for the pattern. Draw what comes next.

Name _____

Patterns Practice *(cont.)*

Look for the pattern. Draw what comes next.

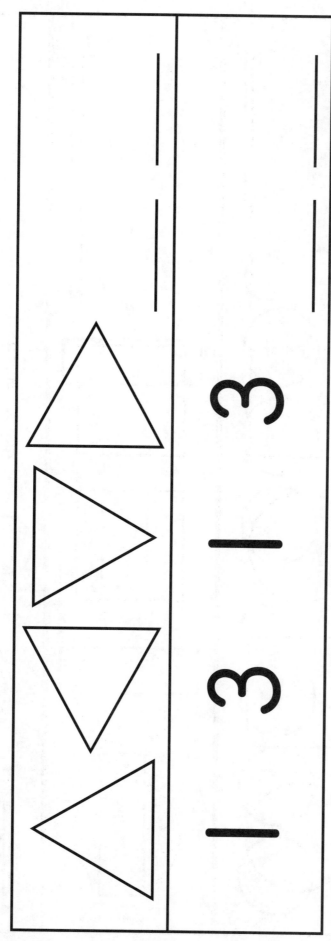

Make your own pattern, using different colors, numbers, or shapes.

Patterns Practice *(cont.)*

Look for the pattern. Draw what comes next.

Name

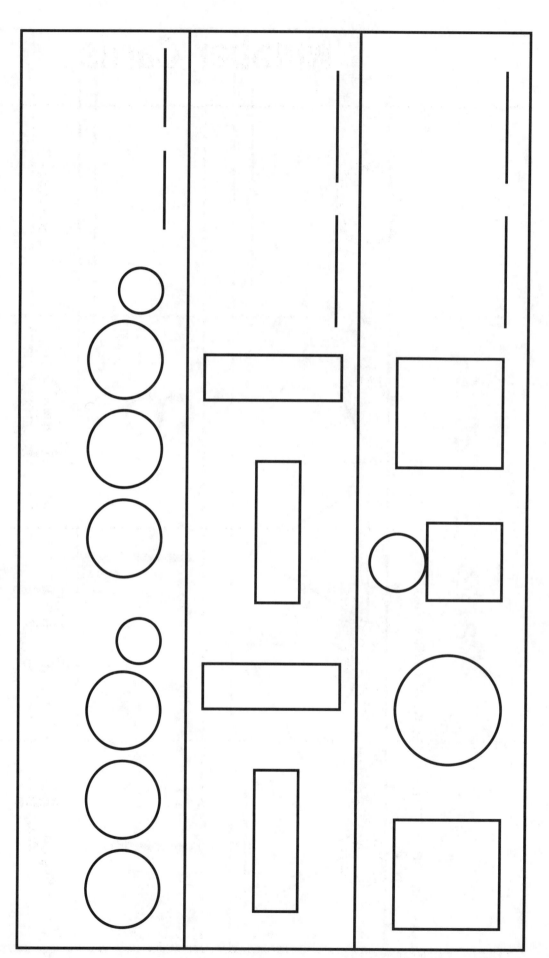

Number Cards

0	1
2	3
4	5
6	7

Number Cards *(cont.)*

8	9
10	11
12	13
14	15

Number Cards *(cont.)*

16	17
18	19
20	21
22	23

Number Cards *(cont.)*

24	25
26	27
28	29
30	35

Number Cards *(cont.)*

45	55
65	75
85	95
40	50

Number Cards *(cont.)*

60	70
80	90
100	200
300	400

184

Number Cards *(cont.)*

500	600
700	800
900	1,000

Please and Thank You

WHAT

Please and *thank you* are probably the most important words we can teach our children when it comes to manners. This lesson focuses on how and when to use the words *please* and *thank you*.

WHY

Every society has a code of etiquette, or manners. In our society, the words *please* and *thank you* are very important. Proper use of these words has become an integral part of good behavior. Activities focusing on the words *please* and *thank you* can provide children practice with:

- speaking
- applying rules of etiquette
- understanding social situations
- applying reasoning skills

HOW

Begin a discussion where you ask children if they have ever heard of the word *please*. Most children will already have some familiarity with the word. To focus on the word, a teacher might have the children say it ten times really fast, really slowly, etc. Depending on what other activities students have done, a teacher might have children figure out how many syllables are in the word, what its beginning sound is, if they can hear any vowels, etc.

As a visual aid, a teacher can hold up the word *please* (page 189). The teacher can have children form the letters of the word with their entire bodies. A teacher may also choose to count the number of letters in the word, as well as the number of vowels.

Next, ask children when they would say *please*. A teacher might direct the children by saying:

"You want to ask someone for some juice. How would you do it?"

"You need to know where something is (book, bathroom, etc.). How would you do it?"

"You want to do something (go to the beach, to play with a friend, etc.). How would you ask?"

Explain to children that we use the word *please* because it is a "magic" word. It makes people feel good. Ask them if they can think of another word that we use that makes people feel good. If children do not come up with *thank you* on their own, lead them to it by saying, "Someone just gave me a new ball. What do I say?"

Follow the same steps that you did with the word *please* using the words *thank you*. Contrast, if desired, your answers, such as how many letters, vowels, etc., to the word *please*.

Finally, tell the children that they are going to be Please and Thank You Detectives. They have to figure out when to say these words, and then they have to say them. Make up silly and wild situations to entertain the children. Vary them with more realistic scenarios.

Please and Thank You *(cont.)*

HOW *(cont.)*

These are some sample questions:

- An octopus wants to take you to dinner. Do you say, "No, thank you," or "Yes, please"?

- You have just been given a new book. Do you say, "please," or "thank you"?

- Want to jump out of an airplane? Do you say, "No, thank you," or "Yes, please"?

- You need to know where the bathroom is. When you ask, would you start with a "please" or a "thank you"?

- You go to bed, and you find an enormous dinosaur on it. Do you say, "Please move over," or "Thank you, move over"?

- You have been offered rhinoceros toenails to eat. Do you say, "Yes, please," or "No, thank you"?

- You want to use some crayons that a tiger is using. Do you say, "Please, will you share?" or "Thank you, we will share"? What do you say if the tiger shares with you: "Please," or "Thank you"?

There will be many times over the school year that a child forgets to use the words *please* and *thank you*. When this happens, rather than asking the child to say them, a teacher can continue to develop reasoning skills by saying, "You forgot to say a word that makes me feel good. You are smart. Do you think it is 'please' or 'thank you'?"

HANDS-ON PRACTICE

Make enough copies of the Please and Thank You Practice page (page 189) for each child. Have them trace the words *please* and *thank you*. Children can color and decorate the cards, too.

CLASS EXTENSIONS

A teacher can continue with situations where a child has to be a Please and Thank You Detective, but with a twist. Instead of having them speak the word, children respond by holding up the proper card. For example, if a child is asked if he or she wants to be pushed off his or her bike, the children's response should be to yell out, "No!" and then hold up the card with the word *thank you* printed on it.

A teacher may also choose to make copies of the alphabet and vowel cards (pages 23–27 and 90–91) of the letters that make up the words *please* and *thank you*. Children can then color or trace these letters, arrange them in the right order, and paste them onto a piece of paper. They can use the Please and Thank You Practice page (page 189) to check their spelling.

HOME PAGE

Hello,

Today we talked about the words *please* and *thank you*. We picked which words—*please* or *thank you*—would fit in different situations.

Practice with applying please and thank you helps a child to understand social situations and helps him or her develop good manners.

Entertain your child by having him or her be a Please and Thank You Detective. Give him or her a situation where he or she has to choose which words to say, *please* or *thank you*.

These are some silly situations that might be used:

Your brother wants you to hold a toad in your pocket. Do you say, "Yes, please," or "No, thank you"?

A dinosaur just gave you a ride on his back. Do you say, "Please," or "Thank you"?

Someone is handing out pink and purple ice cream. Do you say, "Yes, please," or "No, thank you"?

You want to go to the moon. Do you say, "Please, take me to the moon," or "Thank you, take me to the moon"?

Note: There will be many times a child forgets to use the words *please* and *thank you*. When this happens, sometimes, rather than asking the child to say them, you might say, "You forgot to say a word that makes me feel good. You are smart. Do you think it is 'please' or 'thank you'?"

Have fun!

Please and Thank You Practice

Trace or color the words **please** and **thank you**.

Introductions

WHAT

Introductions are a part of life. One introduces friends to friends, adults (parents, relatives, caregivers) to friends, and friends to adults. This lesson introduces children to the concept of social introductions. It familiarizes children with the etiquette rules involving the order of introductions: who to whom?

WHY

First impressions are important. Often, the first impression comes with introductions. There are social etiquette rules when it comes to how people are introduced to one another. Having children practice and role-play with these rules at an early age enhances and helps develop the following skills:

- awareness of other beings
- accepted social behavior
- ability to differentiate sex and age
- speaking confidence

HOW

Two basic rules of introduction will be addressed. The first deals with gender. When one is introducing a girl to a boy, the girl's name is spoken first. For example, "Sarah, this is my friend, Ben."

The second rule deals with age. Social etiquette dictates that one introduces the younger person to the older, but says the name of the older person first. For example, if a child is introducing an adult to his or her friend, the appropriate order is to say, "Mom (older person), this is my friend, Alex (younger person)."

Engage children in a discussion about who they know. Ask them how they met these people and how they learned their names. At this point, you might want to have children speak their own names or the names of those next to them.

Explain to children that just as there are rules about how to behave in movie theaters, in school, and while eating, there are rules that we can follow when we introduce two people to each other. When we introduce someone to someone else, we are helping these people meet and learn each other's names.

Ask children when they might have to introduce someone to someone else (when a friend comes over to your home and you need to introduce him or her to your caregiver, when you want one friend to meet another friend.)

Next, ask the children who the boys and girls are in the room. Next, ask them who are the adults and who are the children. When the children come up with the correct responses, enthusiastically inform them that they already know most of the rules of introduction because what is important is being able to tell girls from boys, as well as who is older.

Introductions *(cont.)*

HOW *(cont.)*

Practice the "girl to boy" rule first. Tell the children that if they are introducing a girl to a boy, they should say the name of the girl first. Give several examples, using the names of the students. "Maria, this is Jon," "Tanya, this is Alfredo."

Have the children take turns introducing two people to each other. Once the children are familiar with saying the girl's name first, go on to the second rule. It should be noted that both rules do not have to be taught on the same day. Some teachers may prefer to work on the girl's name being said first for a day or week before going on to introductions that take age into account.

Inform the children that they know how to introduce girls to boys; they are ready for the second rule— the one that deals with age. Ask them to guess the order. "If you are introducing your friend to your caregiver, do you introduce your caregiver to your friend or your friend to your caregiver?"

Explain that rules of etiquette state that you introduce your friend to the caregiver, parent, or older person, but that you say your caregiver's name first. In other words, you introduce young to old, but you say the older person's name first. Provide lots of examples, using names of children in the class: "Mom, this is my friend, Cara," "Dad, this is my friend, Franklin," "Grandpa, this is my friend, Marissa," "Mrs. Chan, this is my friend, Montana." Have children practice introducing fellow students to the adults in the class.

HANDS-ON PRACTICE

Engage in role-playing. Bring in props, such as a wig, cane, suit jacket, briefcase, or other occupational accessories, that make a child look older. Once the child is dressed, have other children introduce their friends. Don't forget that one can make up very silly names for the dressed-up children!

Have children color the paper figures (pages 193–196). If desired, children can glue the figures onto sticks so that they can be used as puppets. Or, children can make puppets by gluing or taping the paper figures onto small paper bags. Have children practice introducing the puppets to each other.

CLASS EXTENSIONS

Every time there is a guest speaker, parent or caretaker volunteer throughout the year, practice with the chosen or related child ahead of time how he or she will introduce the speaker to the class. When the speaker arrives, have the designated child introduce the speaker.

When books are read to the class, part of the following discussion can focus on "what if" introductions. Name characters and ask who would introduce whom.

HOME PAGE

Hello,

Today we talked about introductions. We learned that when one is introducing a girl to a boy, one says the girl's name first. For example, "Sarah, this is Ryan."

We also learned that when one is introducing a friend to one's caregiver (or someone older), one introduces the friend to one's caregiver, but says the caregiver's name first. For example, "Mom, this is my friend, Ted," and, "Mr. Lopez, this is my friend, Lita."

This activity helps a child become familiar with the rules of social etiquette. It provides practice for social situations.

Practice introductions by having your child introduce his or her friends to you or other adults when you meet. Don't forget to introduce your child to your friends!

"_____ (your friend's name), this is _____ (child's name)."

Have fun!

Introductions Practice

Cut out and color the figure. You may paste the figure onto a stick or a paper bag to use it as a puppet.

Introductions Practice (cont.)

Cut out and color the figure. You may paste the figure onto a stick or a paper bag to use it as a puppet.

Introductions Practice *(cont.)*

Cut out and color the figure. You may paste the figure onto a stick or a paper bag to use it as a puppet.

Introductions Practice *(cont.)*

Cut out and color the figure. You may paste the figure onto a stick or a paper bag to use it as a puppet.

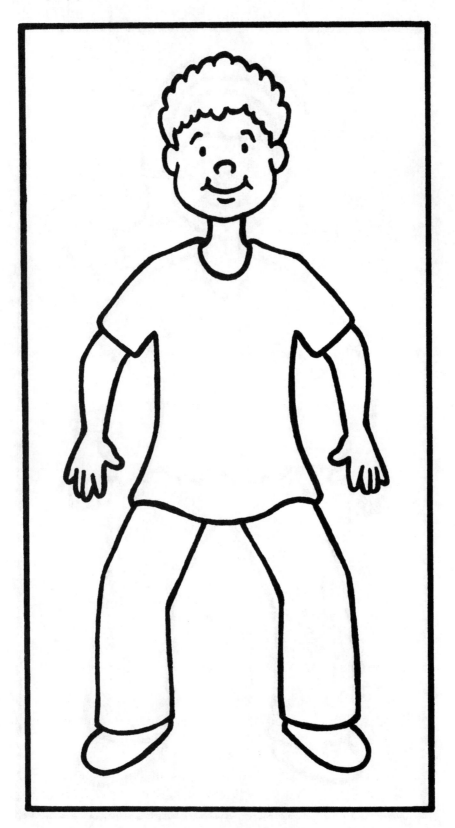

Handshaking

WHAT

It is the social convention in many countries to shake hands when one is introduced to another person. There are etiquette rules about the proper way to shake a person's hand. This activity focuses on handshaking and the proper way to practice it.

WHY

Everyone is more comfortable in social situations if he or she knows how to behave properly. Engaging children in handshaking activities at an early age:

- familiarizes a child with social conventions
- provides practice differentiating between left and right
- provides motor skills practice
- heightens a child's tactile awareness or sense of touch
- increases confidence in social situations

HOW

Engage children in a discussion where you ask them if they have ever seen people shake hands. Ask them if they have noticed when this typically happens. A teacher might suggest these possibilities:

When people are eating breakfast (*no*)	painting a house (*no*)
eating a banana (*no*)	driving a car (*no*)
meeting each other for the first time (*yes*)	saying good-bye (*sometimes*)

Explain that handshaking is done in many countries when two people are introduced to each other or meet each other for the first time.

Next, ask children if they think there are rules about handshaking. After agreeing that there are, ask the children if they think there is a rule about what hand they use to shake. Have the children shake, raise, or wiggle their fingers on their right hands. (A teacher might want to have children guess which hand to use first by some sort of physical motion.) Explain that one always uses one's right hand unless one is disabled. In that case, it is appropriate to use the left hand.

Have the children put their hands out and stretch out their fingers. Ask them to find their thumbs and their first or pointer fingers. With the finger and thumb still stretched out, have the children feel the skin or "web" between the digits.

Next, have children clasp their own hands together by having them touch the web of the right hand to the web of the left hand between the thumb and the pointer finger. Explain that when people shake hands, one not only uses the right hand, but that one shakes "web to web."

The last rule to bring up is that a good handshake is firm. Children may not know exactly what firm feels like, so a teacher might want to exaggerate a limp handshake, or one where little effort is exerted.

Handshaking *(cont.)*

HOW *(cont.)*

Start practicing right away by shaking the hands of the children and having them shake yours. Have the children shake hands with each other.

HANDS-ON PRACTICE

Make copies of the outlined hands (page 200) for each child. (You may have children trace their own hands.) Cut out the hands (a teacher may want to do this before they are decorated). Next, have the children fit the hands together web to web and paste them on another sheet of paper.

Children will also enjoy a game where they are Handshake Detectives. Have one child make a mistake on purpose. The other child has to figure out whether the mistake was:

- not using the right hand
- not going "web to web"
- not firm

CLASS EXTENSIONS

Handshaking is an activity that can be done throughout the year at times when children meet guest speakers.

Bring up the whole idea of "Let's make a deal," and "Let's shake on it." Discuss how in certain countries and societies, people shake hands to show that they agree with each other. The handshake shows that they will keep their word about what was agreed upon. Children might be encouraged to shake hands in class when they agree to share, to take turns, not to fight, etc.

If a teacher wish, he or she can give the children one more rule. This rule concerns cold or wet hands. In these cases, you should not shake hands. A teacher might want to demonstrate to children what it feels like to shake a wet or cold hand. (This can be done by touching a cold washcloth first or by touching a surgical or dishwashing glove that has been filled with water and frozen.)

Explain that if a child is at a party, he or she should always hold a glass in the left hand. This way, if he or she is introduced to someone and needs to shake a hand, the right hand will be dry and warm. One might want to have the children hold paper cups of ice so that they can feel how it makes their hands feel cold. It should be noted that this rule is outside the realm of the preschool world, and it should only be introduced if students are enjoying handshaking immensely and want more fun. In truth, preschool children will enjoy making their hands feel cold more than the handshaking!

HOME PAGE

Hello,

Today we practiced shaking hands. We worked on shaking with our right hands, using a firm grip, and meeting web (the skin of the finger between the thumb and pointer finger) to web.

This activity helps a child become familiar with and gain confidence in social interactions. It provides practice differentiating between left and right. It helps a child begin to be aware of how things feel and control his or her motor movements appropriately.

Asking your child to shake hands provides great practice and fun. Play Handshake Detective where one person has to make a mistake—he or she uses the left hand, does not go web to web, or has a limp clasp. The other person has to detect what is wrong.

Have fun!

Handshaking Practice

Cut out and color the hands. Put them together so the thumb and the first finger are "web to web." Paste the hands on a piece of paper.

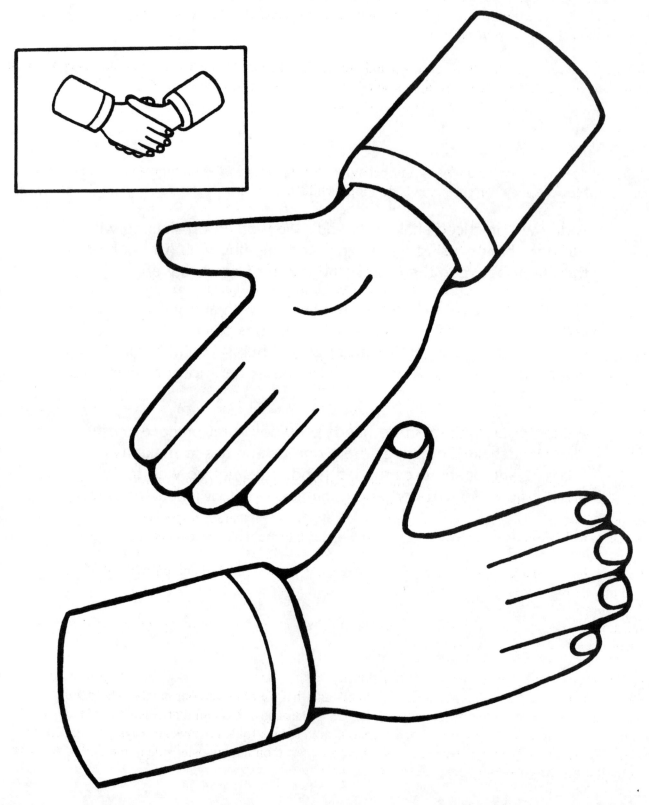

Napkin Placement

WHAT

When one sets a table, the napkin is typically placed on the left side of the plate. It is folded into a rectangle with the exposed side facing the right (near the plate). When you sit down, you open the napkin and place it on your lap.

What do you do if you ask to be excused and are leaving the table momentarily, but plan to come back to finish eating? If you are returning to the table, place your napkin on the seat of the chair. If you are finished, place the napkin to the right of your plate.

WHY

We are judged in social situations by our behavior. Practicing the rules of etiquette, especially that of napkin placement at an early age, helps develop a child's:

- awareness of nonverbal cues
- directional sense (left vs. right)
- ability to differentiate between ending and ongoing situations
- confidence in social situations because of familiarity with etiquette rules

HOW

Show children several different napkins (cloth and paper, if possible) and ask them if they know what they are and what their purpose is.

Next, ask the children where napkins are supposed to be placed while you are eating. (If the teacher desires, he or she can place a napkin on his or her head, arm, foot, and finally lap, asking, "Is this where a napkin goes?")

Bring up a situation where you are eating and need to leave the table (a need for the restroom, a gorilla at the window that needs to be told that no one is able to play, a lion that needs to be told that he cannot be pushed on the swing until after the meal, etc.). Explain that there is a special way—where you do not have to talk—to show that you will be coming back to the table to finish eating.

Explain that the napkin goes to the right of the plate if you are finished and on the seat of the chair if you are coming back.

Demonstrate placing the napkin on the seat of the chair and to the right of a plate several times, asking each time what one's intentions are.

Children may have a difficult time with the direction of "right." Have children hold up their hands. Discuss that everyone has a right and a left hand, and that we often use our hands to help with directions. Ask the children to shake or raise their right hands. Explain that when the table is set, the napkin usually goes on the left side. (Exceptions are napkins folded in special ways and placed on plates, typically at formal restaurants.) Napkins are placed on the opposite side at the end of the meal as they were at the beginning.

Napkin Placement *(cont.)*

HANDS-ON PRACTICE

Children may color paper towels (paper towels are often easier to color than actual paper napkins) or paper napkins. These decorated napkins or ordinary paper napkins can be used at every snack time as well as incorporated into a game.

The game starts with children sitting at the table, napkins placed on their laps. The teacher would then call out situations where the children would have to rise and place their napkins appropriately. Because this game involves the physical motion of getting up and down, it is sometimes a good method to distract children who are finding it difficult to sit quietly. The teacher might call out entertaining comments filled with humor and exaggeration. For example,

> "You ate six bags of rice, twenty sandwiches, and four cakes. You feel so full that you think your stomach is going to burst. Where are you going to put your napkin when you say excuse me and get up?"

> "Oh dear. There is a dinosaur at the door. It wants to play soccer with you, but you are not finished eating. Where do you put your napkin while you go tell it to come back later?"

> "You need to excuse yourself for a moment because you see a snake crawling up your Auntie's chair, and you think you should pick up the snake and carry it outside. You also know that there is going to be ice cream for dessert. Where are you going to place your napkin?"

CLASS EXTENSIONS

Make copies of the Napkin Placement Practice page (page 204). Ask children to decide on which side of the plate the napkin goes. Have children draw a colored napkin on the left side of the plate. Or, have children paste a napkin they have decorated on the left side of the plate.

To practice motor skills, a teacher may choose to extend this lesson with folding. He or she can have students fold sheets of paper or napkins into rectangles. Students can feel and look at the sides with the folds versus the sides with the exposed edges. Practice placing the sides with the exposed edges toward the plate. Set up a Search Mission, where students search for napkins that are placed with the edges out rather than in.

Note: One might also want to mention to children that the rules of etiquette state that one should never embarrass other people or make them feel bad. If children notice that someone else does not place his or her napkin on the lap, he or she should not be corrected. What children should do is just look down and check that they remembered to put their own napkins in the right place.

HOME PAGE

Hello,

Today we talked about using napkins and where to place them while we eat. We also talked about where napkins go at the end of the meal, as well as where they go if one needs to leave the table but is coming back to finish eating.

This activity introduces a child to etiquette rules and helps develop a child's awareness of nonverbal cues and directional sense. It helps a child learn to differentiate between ending and ongoing situations.

A napkin is typically placed on the left side of the plate. It is folded into a rectangle with the exposed edge facing the right. When one sits down, one opens the napkin and places it on one's lap.

When one is finished eating, the napkin is placed to the right of one's plate. If one is returning to the table after momentarily excusing oneself, one places the napkin on the seat of one's chair.

Have your child place napkins at the dinner table. Ask him or her where the napkin should go if one wants to return to the table to eat.

Have fun!

Name _____

Napkin Placement Practice

Draw a napkin where it belongs in this picture.

Table Setting Diagram

Use the reference page for proper napkin placement.

Sipping Soup

WHAT

The rules of etiquette state that when dipping your soup spoon into a soup bowl, the scooping motion should be done in the direction away from your body. This activity focuses on the proper way to sip soup.

WHY

Eating is often a social situation. Good manners add to the pleasure. Practicing sipping soup provides a manipulative and entertaining way to reinforce dining etiquette rules. It helps to reduce the number of soup spills on one's clothes, while strengthening a child's:

- sense of direction (away from vs. toward)
- confidence in social situations because of familiarity with etiquette rules
- coordination

HOW

First, ask the children if they know what soup is and if they can name their favorite kind. Then ask them what soup is served in (*a bowl*) and what utensil (*a spoon*) they use to sip it.

Second, explain that just as there are rules for standing in line, what age one has to be to drive a car, and paying for store items, there are rules—called *etiquette*—about behavior. *Etiquette* is good manners. It is rules that society has set up for the proper way to behave when dealing with other people.

Ask children if they can think of some rules of etiquette or how to behave. (*Saying, "How do you do,"* *"thank you," and "excuse me"; taking off one's hat when one enters a room if one is male; shaking hands; etc.*)

Next, ask children if they can think of rules for eating. (*Not eating with your hands, not eating with your mouth open, not talking with your mouth full, not spitting out your food,* etc.) Explain that etiquette rules are sometimes different in other countries and that business people who travel take lessons in how to be polite in other countries. For example, it is polite to slurp your soup in some cultures, while in others it is inappropriate.

Explain that today's etiquette lesson is on how to sip soup. Ask children to demonstrate how they would sip soup. Then ask them if they scoop the spoon toward their bodies or away from their bodies. Demonstrate and have the children follow the motion of scooping soup away from the body. Ask them why it might be cleaner to scoop soup away from yourself (*less likely to spill on one's shirt!*).

Lastly, have the children repeat this rhyme several times.

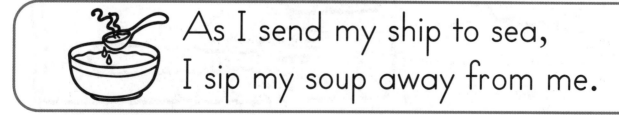

As I send my ship to sea,
I sip my soup away from me.

Sipping Soup *(cont.)*

HANDS-ON PRACTICE

If soup is served for a snack, it provides real-life practice, but soup is not a typical snack dish for many preschools. Engage the children in a role-play where they practice with water or simply mime the motions.

Play a Soup Sipper Detective game where one motions sipping soup and asks the children to detect if one is sipping in the right direction. Vary this game by having the children mime sipping soup, and the appointed Soup Sipper Detective has to spot the child who is using the wrong motion.

Note: One might also want to mention to children that the rules of etiquette state that one should not embarrass other people or make them feel bad. If they notice someone sipping soup incorrectly, they should not yell it out. Instead, they should just quietly check themselves to make sure that they are not forgetting to move their spoons away from themselves.

CLASS EXTENSIONS

Find a simple recipe for soup that works for your class. This recipe can be for a cold or warm soup, or more like a punch where different fruit juices are combined. Have children bring in different ingredients. Sip and savor!

One may also engage children in a sipping experiment. Using plain water to prevent stains, have children sip soup scooping in the wrong direction. Then, have them sip soup with the right motion, scooping the liquid away from them. See which way produces more spills.

HOME PAGE

Hello,

Today we covered the etiquette of sipping soup and practiced scooping it from one's bowl away from one's body.

This activity strengthens a child's coordination and sense of direction (away versus toward). It develops table manners, as well as helps a child learn that there are codes of behavior to be followed. Perhaps most importantly, it helps to reduce the number of soup spills on a child's clothes!

Help your child remember which direction to sip soup with this rhyme:

 As I send my ship to sea,

I sip my soup away from me.

Have fun!

Where's My Water?

WHAT

Water glasses are typically placed above your silverware and to the right of your plate. This lesson teaches a child where to place a water glass.

WHY

When you sit down at a large table set for a great number of people, you might not be able to tell which water glass is yours. There are too many glasses, all close together! You do not want to take the glass of the person sitting to the left, for it can set off an embarrassing chain reaction where one person is left without a glass. Practicing recognizing where one's water glass is placed helps to develop a child's:

- directional sense (left vs. right)
- confidence in social situations because of familiarity with etiquette rules
- table-setting skills

HOW

A teacher can teach this lesson at a table or in a circle, with everyone sitting on the floor. Each child should be given a paper cup and asked to place it in front of him or her. Next, the teacher should ask the children if they have ever eaten in large groups at one table. Discuss how this would mean that there are lots of plates, utensils, and glasses. Ask them how they would know which glass is their own, especially if it seems that there is one on both sides of their plates. At this point, have the children pick up their cups. Were there any mistakes?

Explain that there are rules about where glasses are set on a table to keep mistakes from happening. A teacher might want to bring up funny situations such as:

"Would you like to drink out of the water glass of the silly squirrel sitting next to you?"

"Would you like to drink out of the water glass of the dog that hasn't brushed his teeth?"

"Would you like to drink out of the water glass of the elephant that forgot to wipe his nose?"

Explain and demonstrate that glasses are placed to one's right. Have children pick up their glasses several times and place them to their right.

Children may have a difficult time with the direction of "right." Have children hold up their hands. Discuss that everyone has a right and a left hand and that we often use our hands to help with directions. Ask the children to shake or raise their right hands. Explain that many people use their right hand to help them remember which side "right" goes on. If you have already practiced the napkin placement lesson, you can tell children that both the napkin and the water glass go on the right when one is finished eating.

Where's My Water? *(cont.)*

HOW *(cont.)*

Talk about how some people use this rhyme as a reminder as to how glasses and extra plates for bread and butter or salad are placed around the big plate.

Lefty Lumpy, Righty Runny.

A teacher might want to discuss how water and other liquids are runny, and how breads and salads are lumpy in comparison. Have children repeat this rhyme several times until they are comfortable with it.

Once again, have children place their cups in front of them, to the right. Next, have the children close their eyes and reach for their cups. Remind children to reach toward the right. Were there any mistakes?

HANDS-ON PRACTICE

Make copies for each child of the Where's My Water? Practice pages (pages 212–213). Have children color and decorate the pages. Next, have children cut out and paste the glasses they colored on the right side and above the silverware on the page with the plate.

CLASS EXTENSIONS

Children can also color paper cups and practice placing them on the right side of where they sit to eat. As an alternative exercise, a teacher can set a table with cups that look exactly alike and then request that the students figure out which one is theirs. This game can also be played where one cup is missing, and the children have to figure out whose cup is missing from the table.

One can also have children set up glasses for stuffed animals that have been arranged around a table. Remove one glass and have the children figure out which animal is missing a glass.

Note: One might also want to mention to children that the rules of etiquette state that one should not embarrass other people or make them feel bad. If they notice that someone has taken their water glass, they should politely and quietly ask their host or hostess for another one.

HOME PAGE

Hello,

Today we talked about where one's cup or glass is placed at the table. Glasses are typically placed above one's silverware and to the right of one's plate.

This activity helps develop a child's directional sense (left vs. right) and gives a child practice with the rules of etiquette.

Have your child practice placing water glasses on the right side of the plate when he or she helps set the table.

We used the following rhyme to help us remember. The "lumpy" refers to solid foods, or the bread plate or salad plate. "Runny" refers to liquids, or drinks.

> Lefty Lumpy, Righty Runny.

Have fun!

Name _____

Where's My Water? Practice

Where is the missing water glass? Draw the missing water glass, or color and cut out a water glass and paste it on the table.

Name _____

Where's My Water? Practice *(cont.)*

Which water glass do you like? Pick a water glass, color it, cut it out, and paste it where it belongs on the picture of the table.

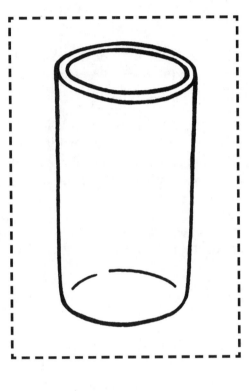

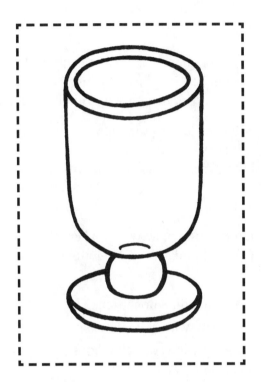

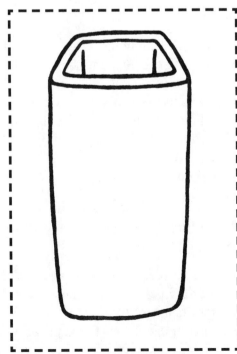

Silverware—Outside In

WHAT

Dining etiquette follows specific rules when it comes to how a table is set and in which order silverware is used. This lesson focuses on how to place silverware on the table and in which order it should be used.

WHY

Our rules of etiquette state that when a table is set, forks are placed on the left side of the plate. Knives, with the knife blade facing inward, and spoons are placed on the right. The exception is when there is only a fork being used. In this case, the fork is placed to the right of the plate.

When it comes to the order in which silverware should be used, the easy rule is "Outside in." One picks up the silverware farthest away from the plate and next uses the pieces that go increasingly in toward the plate. If soup was the first course, for example, the soup spoon would be placed on the right-hand side of the plate, farthest from the inside. The knife would be placed between the plate and the spoon.

Engaging children in activities where they set tables and practice choosing a utensil with which to eat provides a manipulative and entertaining way to reinforce dining etiquette rules while strengthening a child's:

- spatial and directional sense (outside to inside, left vs. right)
- familiarity with eating utensils
- confidence in social situations because of familiarity with etiquette rules
- table-setting skills

HOW

Engage the children in a discussion where the names and purpose of eating utensils are reviewed. For example, hold up a plate (paper or plastic) and ask the children what it is called and what it is for. If children are not yet sure of the word *plate*, have them repeat the word while engaging in several activities such as speaking as fast as they can, as loudly as they can, and as softly as they can. A good rule of thumb is saying the word five times for each activity. It should be fairly easy for children to bring up that plates are used to put food on, but if they need directing, ask, "And so what do I do with this plate? Do I wear it on my head? Do I put it on my foot? Do I drive a car with it? Do I put food on it?" Repeat this same type of activity with forks, spoons, and knives.

Once the names have been reviewed, a teacher can ask children to visualize or picture the items in their heads. For example, a teacher can say, "Close your eyes. Think of a plate." Ask the children to open their eyes and hold up a plate. Ask, "Is this what you pictured?"

At this time, a teacher should hand out to each child a plastic or paper plate and one knife, two spoons, and two forks. If a teacher desires, he or she can engage the children in an activity where they close their eyes, pick up one item, and guess what it is. If a teacher does not wish to use plastic utensils, he or she can make copies of the Silverware—Outside In Practice page (page 218). These paper utensils can be cut out and laminated for teaching purposes.

Silverware—Outside In *(cont.)*

HOW *(cont.)*

Next, bring up that just as there are rules for how we behave, drive, and dress, there are rules about how we set the table and how we use our silverware.

Explain that the most important thing to remember is outside in. Even though children will not yet know what this means, have them repeat it several times, incorporating several activities such as jumping up, with eyes closed, as fast as they can, etc. Place a plate in front of you, with utensils appropriately placed around it. Explain that sometimes we eat lots of different foods, and sometimes we want a clean fork or spoon. For example, we don't want to use the same fork for cake that we used for macaroni and cheese. So how do we know which fork to use? Outside in!

Point to the fork on the outside, and say, "This would be the fork for the macaroni and cheese, and this would be the fork for the dessert."

Some children will bring up that they rarely see more than one fork or knife. Tell them they have good eyes, and that they are right. You just want them to know the rules if they are ever in a situation where there is lots of silverware because all different types of things are being eaten.

Finally, ask the children if they noticed something about what sides the silverware went on. Explain to them that forks go on the left, and knives and spoons go on the right. Ask them, too, if they notice anything about the direction of the knife. Point out to them that the blade faces the plate.

Next, have them set their own places in front of them. When their places are set, pretend to eat. Call out,

"Um, pea soup first. Which piece of silverware do I use?"
(When the silverware is used, have children place it behind them.)

"Oh, a salad comes next. Which piece of silverware do I use?"

"Um, a big piece of fish. Which two pieces of silverware do I use?"

Silverware–Outside In *(cont.)*

HANDS-ON PRACTICE

Make a copy for each child of the Silverware–Outside In Practice pages (pages 218–219). A teacher may choose to have the children draw the silverware on the outlined table setting (page 219). Or, he or she may have children color, cut out, and paste the silverware pieces (page 218) in the appropriate places on the place setting.

Children can also set their own places for snack time. If silverware is not being used, children can place their paper utensils alongside their plates.

CLASS EXTENSION

Set up an imaginary meal that you might eat if you were a particular character from a book. For example, Jack, from *Jack in the Beanstalk,* would have a meal of bean soup, bean salad, bean steak, and bean pie. Pretend to eat it.

One could be Sam-I-Am from Dr. Seuss's *Green Eggs and Ham.* Which utensils would be used to eat green eggs and ham?

One could be Goldilocks, eating porridge. What type of porridge would you serve? Would you set her table with three different spoons of different sizes? Which spoon would be placed so it is used first, second, and third?

One could be Peter Rabbit. His meal could be made up of things found in a garden. He might eat carrot soup, lettuce pie, and a radish sandwich. Which kind of utensils would you need?

One could be King Midas where everything he touches is turned to gold. What foods could you serve that are gold colored?

HOME PAGE

Hello,

Today we talked about silverware (tableware). We practiced identifying and pronouncing the words *plates, forks, spoons,* and *knives.* We also practiced basic table setting. We introduced the rule "outside in" using silverware farthest out from the plate first, then using the pieces that go increasingly in toward the plate.

This activity familiarizes a child with eating utensils and proper dining etiquette. It also helps to develop a child's spatial and directional sense (outside to inside, left vs. right).

Have your child practice by having him or her help set the table.

Engage your child in fun discussions with questions such as:

"An elephant is coming to eat ice cream and soup. How many spoons will it need? (*two*) Should the spoon on the outside, farthest away from the plate, be used for the ice cream or the soup?" (*If the soup is eaten first, the spoon for the soup will be the outside spoon, farthest from the plate.*)

"A tiger comes to join the elephant. The tiger says, 'I am eating ice cream first.' You don't want to argue with the tiger, so you give him the ice cream first. Does the tiger use the spoon on the outside, the one farthest from the plate, or the one closest to the plate?" (*The tiger uses the spoon on the outside, farthest from the plate.*)

"The Princess invites you to lunch. You want to remember your manners. A salad made with old turnip leaves and pea slices is brought to you first. Which piece of silverware do you use to eat?" (*You use the outside fork.*)

Have fun!

Silverware–Outside In Practice

Color and cut out the silverware.

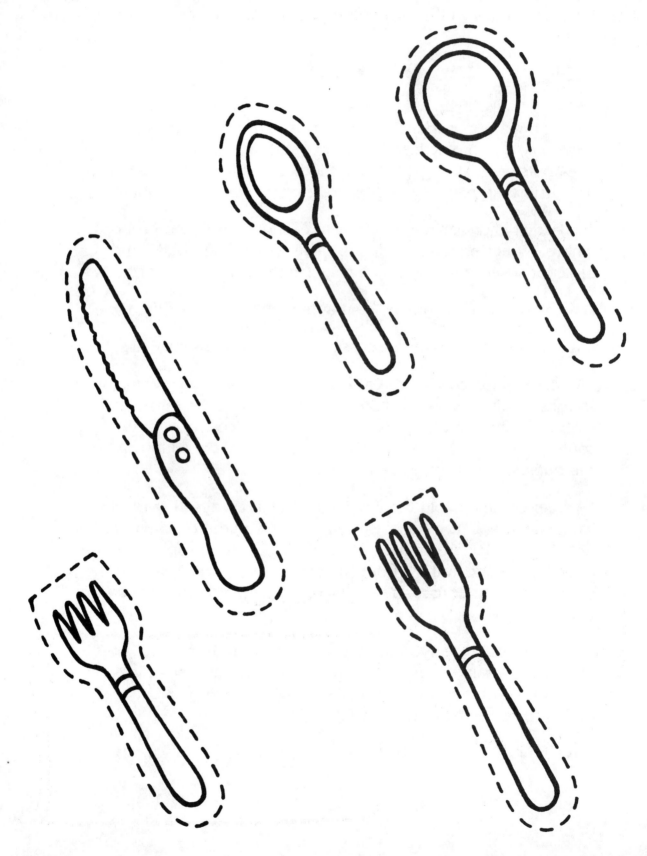

Silverware–Outside In Practice *(cont.)*

Where is the missing silverware? Draw the missing silverware, placing it where it should go. Or, paste on the silverware you colored and cut out from the first practice page.

Talking with Silverware

WHAT

Silverware has a language of its own. Dining etiquette follows specific rules, as do other aspects of proper social behavior. This lesson focuses on the proper placement of silverware when one has finished eating.

WHY

Our rules of etiquette state that when one is finished eating, one should place one's fork and knife on top of the plate on the right side. If one pictures a clock on one's plate, the knife and fork should be side-by-side, tips at the center of the plate, ends lying between where the numbers three and four would be found.

Playing "I am done" versus "I am only resting" silverware games provides a manipulative and entertaining way to reinforce dining etiquette rules while strengthening a child's abilities in:

- nonverbal language skills
- spatial and directional sense (top vs. bottom, left vs. right)
- knowledge of number placement on a clock
- his or her sense of completion versus an activity that is still in process
- understanding social situations because of familiarity with etiquette rules

HOW

After reviewing the shapes and names of the knife and fork, tell children that they can talk without words. They can use their silverware to let people know that they are just resting from eating, or that they are still eating. Demonstrate silverware placement that signifies whether one is finished or that one is resting. One may use laminated copies of the silverware (page 218) or use plastic silverware to demonstrate where the silverware should be placed.

Next, engage children in a Detective Game where they have to answer, "Finished!" (or "all finished," "done," etc.) or "Not finished!" (or "still eating," etc.) by placing silverware on a plate.

Place silverware on a plate at a variety of times, such as 12, 6, 9, and 3 o'clock. Have children call out the appropriate responses. Ask engaging questions as you place the silverware on the plate, such as:

"Am I finished, or do you think I could eat a thousand more peas?"

"Do you think I am going to ask for another brownie or some more rice?"

"I left the table so that I could blow my nose. When I left the table, I put my fork at 9:00 and my knife at 3:00. What silent message did I tell the waiter— "I'm coming back so don't take my plate, or 'Go ahead and clear my plate. I'm finished.'"

Talking with Silverware *(cont.)*

HOW *(cont.)*

Introduce or reinforce the concepts of left and right, top and bottom, and clock number alignment by one's questions and answers.

"I am going to rest my silverware across the top of my plate. Am I finished, or am I going to ask for seconds?"

"The baby rhinoceros that came for dinner put his silverware on the left side of the plate. Is that the side that tells us he has finished eating?"

"An octopus tentacle has just been put on your plate. Do you think you will put your silverware on the right bottom of your plate or the right top of your plate?"

HANDS-ON PRACTICE

Have children color and cut out paper silverware and plates (pages 218 and 223). They can place their silverware in various positions, signaling whether they are finished eating or merely resting. A teacher may choose to play a game where real, silly, and nonfoods are called out. Children choose where to place their silverware, signaling that they would eat it, or that they are finished eating. For example, a teacher could call out,

"I have oatmeal cookies. Anyone still hungry?"

"Fried elephant toes. Anyone still hungry?"

"Carrots. Anyone still hungry?"

"Old bicycle wheels. Anyone still hungry?"

"Shoes and socks. Anyone still hungry?"

"Snack crackers. Anyone still hungry?"

CLASS EXTENSION

Discuss and look for other nonverbal signs or cues. For example, how does a dog let one know it wants to go outside? What does it mean when there is a picture of a cigarette with an X through it? How can you tell if someone is unhappy or happy? How do you motion for someone to stop or to come closer? How can you say good-bye or hello to someone with your hand?

Hello,

Today we worked on where you put your silverware when finished eating. If you picture a clock on your plate, the knife and fork should be side-by-side, tips at the center of the plate, ends lying between where the numbers three and four would be found.

This activity helps develop a child's nonverbal language skills, spatial and directional sense (top vs. bottom, left vs. right), and provides an introduction or reinforcement of number placement on a clock. It helps a child differentiate between something that is on-going versus something that is finished. In addition, the familiarity with etiquette rules helps a child behave confidently in social situations.

Every meal is a time when placement of silverware to signify "I'm finished" can be practiced and reinforced. Engage your child with questions such as,

"Do you think I am finished?"

"Do you think your sister is finished?"

"Maria is finished eating, but she didn't say a word. How could I tell?"

"Do you think Kim would like some more?"

"I don't think you are finished. How can I tell?"

Have fun!

Talking with Silverware Practice

Use this plate decorated with clock numbers to help you decide where to place your silverware to show that you are still eating or you are finished.

Animal Families

WHAT

Children are fascinated with family relationships. Who exactly is the father or dad, the mother or mom, the child or baby, the sister, and the brother? Children are also interested in other animals—do they have families, too? This lesson on animal families and the names of individual family members.

WHY

Asking questions about animals' family names captures children's interest while developing a child's ability to:

- group different types of animal families
- differentiate gender (male or female) and age
- increase vocabulary

HOW

Review family names and then engage in playful question-and-answer games.

First, make a teacher set of animal family cards by laminating the Animal Families Practice Cards (pages 228–231). Next, make copies of the animal family cards for each student. Then, lead the class in a discussion.

Animal families can be discussed in any order, but a teacher may choose to separate them into farm (*cow, horse, sheep, pig, chicken, duck,* and *cat*) or wild animals (*fox, deer, bear, whale, kangaroo, swan, goose,* and *rabbit*).

Start with personal family names such as *father, mother, sister, brother,* and *baby.*

Ask or explain which ones are males and females, and which ones are old and young.

Ask individual students to identify what they are.

Introduce one new family. If you are introducing the sheep family, for example, hold up the picture cards (page 229) or pictures from magazines or books.

As each card is held up, have students repeat several times what a father, mother, and baby sheep are called (*ram, ewe, lamb*). Point out that in the sheep family, both the baby girls and boys are called lambs.

When applicable, interject animal noises. With sheep, for example, have the students say, "baaaa."

Animal Families *(cont.)*

HOW *(cont.)*

To reinforce vocabulary and ensure success, your first questions should be entertaining and have obvious answers.

"A ewe is a bathtub or a mother sheep?" *(sheep)*

"A duckling is a mother car or a baby duck?" *(duck)*

"Is a baby bear a cub or a house?" *(cub)*

"Is your kitten a mitten or is it a baby cat?" *(cat)*

"A cygnet is a baby swan or a baby swimming pool?" *(swan)*

"A cob is a father swan or a baby toothbrush?" *(swan)*

"A boomer is a male kangaroo or a chair?" *(kangaroo)*

Questions can be put in varied formats, such as:

"I'm thinking of a calf. Could a calf be a baby rabbit or a baby whale?" *(whale)*

"I'm thinking of a baby animal that says, "baa." Could it be a lamb or a puppy?" *(lamb)*

"I'm thinking of a joey kangaroo. Is a joey kangaroo the daddy, mommy, or baby?" *(baby)*

"I'm thinking of a filly. A filly is a foal, a baby horse, but is a filly a girl baby horse or a boy baby horse?" *(girl)*

Asking questions that require an evaluation of the answer develops reasoning and listening skills.

"I am thinking of a duckling. A duckling is a baby kangaroo. True or false?" *(false—it is a baby duck)*

"I am thinking of a gosling. A gosling is a baby goose. True or false?" *(true)*

"I am thinking of a bull. A bull is a male cow or a male whale. True or false?" *(true)*

"I am thinking of a sow. A sow is a father pig. True or false?" *(false—it is a mother pig)*

"I am thinking of a doe. A doe is a daddy duck. True or false?" *(false—a doe is a female deer or rabbit)*

Questions that require an answer without an answer from which to choose strengthen memory skills and provide vocabulary practice.

A baby goose is called a _____. *(gosling)*

A mother goose is called a _____. *(goose)*

A baby whale is called a _____. *(calf)*

A mother whale is called a _____. *(cow)*

A baby cow is called a _____. *(calf)*

A father cow is called a _____. *(bull)*

A baby horse is called a_____ . *(foal)*

A male foal or male baby horse is called a _____. *(colt)*

Animal Families (cont.)

HANDS-ON PRACTICE

Children can color the animal family cards (pages 228–231). They can pick up or name the family member of each card they touch. They can also answer nonverbally by pointing to or touching the card that corresponds to the teacher's prompt.

CLASS EXTENSION

Look on the Internet, in an encyclopedia, or in animal fact books for family member names of elk, seals, elephants, walruses, dolphins, and other animals.

Farm Animal Families			
	Male	**Female**	**Baby**
cow	bull	cow	calf
horse	stallion	mare	foal (filly/colt)
pig	boar	sow	piglet
sheep	ram	ewe	lamb
goose	gander	goose	gosling
chicken	rooster	hen	chick
duck	drake	duck	duckling

Wild Animal Families			
	Male	**Female**	**Baby**
deer	buck	doe	fawn
rabbit	buck	doe	kit, kitten
bear	boar	sow	cub
whale	bull	cow	calf
kangaroo	boomer	flyer	joey
swan	cob	pen	cygnet

Hello,

Today we talked about animal families. We discussed what the proper names are for the mother, father, and baby in different types of families.

This activity helps a child group different types of animals, differentiate between adult, child, boy, and girl, and increases his or her vocabulary.

Asking questions about animal families is entertaining and a time filler while driving in the car or waiting in lines with your child.

Some of the families we discussed are listed below.

Animal Families			
	Male	**Female**	**Baby**
cow	bull	cow	calf
horse	stallion	mare	foal (filly/colt)
bear	boar	sow	cub
whale	bull	cow	calf
sheep	ram	ewe	lamb
chicken	rooster	hen	chick
kangaroo	boomer	flyer	joey
swan	cob	pen	cygnet

Have fun!

Animal Families Practice Cards

boomer

flyer

joey

buck

doe

fawn

Animal Families Practice Cards *(cont.)*

rooster

hen

chick

ram

ewe

lamb

Animal Families Practice Cards *(cont.)*

stallion

mare

foal
boy = colt   girl = filly

bull

cow

calf

Animal Families Practice Cards *(cont.)*

gander

goose

gosling

buck

doe

kit or kitten

Birds, Trees, and Flowers

WHAT

Most states or provinces have a state or provincial bird, tree, and flower. This lesson focuses on introducing students to the names of these animals and plants.

WHY

Teaching the names of state birds, trees, and flowers can be viewed as a simple exercise. Children learn to identify specific animals and plants. They learn that these animals and plants are special—they have been designated by their states as representatives. This exercise, although seemingly simple and straightforward, can do much more. On the science side, it requires a child to think about the differences among birds, trees, and flowers. It can help a child become aware and develop an interest in the living things around him or her. On the geographical side, it helps a child understand, or reinforces the fact, that the world is divided into specific areas, whether they are state, provincial, or territorial. On the personal side, it can help a child gain a sense of belonging—he or she, just like everyone else who lives with him or her, has a special bird, tree, and flower. Learning about state birds, trees, and flowers provides a child with

- an awareness of other living organisms
- an introduction to how some living things are classified
- an introduction to or reinforcement of geographical areas and names
- a sense of belonging

HOW

A teacher should have a world, country, or state map at hand before this lesson starts, as well as pictures of the state bird, tree, and flower. First, hold up the picture of the bird. Ask children what it is. They should come up with the word *bird.* At this point, ask them to describe some characteristics of birds. If they have trouble coming up with any, you might lead them to the fact that birds fly, have wings, have two legs, have two eyes, have feathers, eat insects, worms, or seeds, lay eggs, and live in nests.

Go on to naming the type of bird that it is. Explain that this is a special type of bird because it is the state bird from your state.

At this point, a teacher should reinforce or introduce some geographical terms. Using the maps, show children where they live and in what country and state they live. Explain that every state has its own special bird, and your state's bird is the one they have just learned the name of. (See lists of birds, trees, and flowers for Canada, Australia, and the United States on pages 233–234.)

Next, tell children that just as each state has a bird, it also has a tree. Ask children for characteristics of trees. Repeat this type of exercise with the state flower. A teacher might want to have children "bloom" like flowers while they repeat the name several times. This would entail sitting scrunched up and then extending legs and arms as if one's petals were unfolding.

Finally, play a game where you point to a child and say, "bird," "tree," or "flower." The child has to call out the applicable name.

Children may come up with questions about other states. Use the list provided to name the other states' birds, trees, and flowers.

Birds, Trees, and Flowers *(cont.)*

HANDS-ON PRACTICE

Have children draw their state bird, tree, and flower.

Make copies of the Birds, Trees, and Flowers Practice pages (pages 236–238) for each child. Children can circle birds, trees, and flowers on the first, second, and third sheets, respectively.

CLASS EXTENSIONS

Have children choose an official class bird, tree, and flower, or official individual birds, trees, and flowers. Official items can be real or made up. Have children name and draw them.

Look up other state birds in a bird guide. Read aloud the descriptions. Decide which bird looks the most interesting, is the largest, the smallest, the most colorful, and the strangest.

Find out if your state has an official mammal or rock.

If any child travels to or has relatives in other states, find the place on the map and then discuss that state's bird, tree, and flower.

Canada

Province	Bird	Tree	Flower
Alberta	great horned owl	lodgepole pine	wildrose
British Columbia	Stellar's jay	western red cedar	Pacific dogwood
Manitoba	great gray owl	white spruce	prairie crocus
New Brunswick	black-capped chickadee	balsam fir	purple violet
Newfoundland	Atlantic puffin	black spruce	pitcher plant
Northwest Territories	gyrfalcon	tamarack	mountain avens
Nova Scotia	osprey	red spruce	mayflower
Nunavut	rock ptarmigan	none	purple saxifrage
Ontario	common loon	eastern white pine	white trillium
Prince Edward Island	blue jay	red oak	lady slipper
Quebec	snowy owl	yellow birch	blue flag
Saskatchewan	sharp-tailed grouse	white birch	red western tiger lily
Yukon Territory	common raven	subalpine fir	fireweed

Australia

Territory	Bird	Flower
Australian Capital Territory	gang-gang cockatoo	royal bluebell
New South Wales	laughing kookaburra	waratah
Northern Territory	wedge-tailed eagle	Sturt's desert rose
Queensland	brolga	Cooktown orchid
South Australia	piping shrike	Sturt's desert pea
Tasmania	green rosella parrot	Tasmaninan blue gum
Victoria	helmeted honeyeater	common heath
Western Australia	black swan	red and green kangaroo paw

Birds, Trees, and Flowers (cont.)

The United States

State	Bird	Tree	Flower
Alabama	yellowhammer	southern pine	camelia
Alaska	willow ptarmigan	sitka spruce	forget-me-not
Arizona	cactus wren	paloverde	saguaro
Arkansas	mockingbird	pine tree	apple blossom
California	California quail	California redwood	golden poppy
Colorado	lark bunting	blue spruce	Rocky Mountain columbine
Connecticut	robin	white oak	mountain laurel
Delaware	blue hen chicken	American holly	peach blossom
Florida	mockingbird	sabal palm	orange blossom
Georgia	brown thrasher	live oak	Cherokee rose
Hawaii	nene	kukui	pua aloalo
Idaho	mountain bluebird	western white pine	syringa
Illinois	cardinal	white oak	native violet
Indiana	cardinal	tulip tree	peony
Iowa	eastern goldfinch	oak	wild rose
Kansas	western meadowlark	cottonwood	sunflower
Kentucky	cardinal	tulip poplar	goldenrod
Louisiana	brown pelican	bald cypress	magnolia
Maine	chickadee	white pine	white pine cone and tassel
Maryland	Baltimore oriole	white oak	black-eyed Susan
Massachusetts	chickadee	American elm	mayflower
Michigan	robin	white pine	apple blossom
Minnesota	common loon	Norway pine	pink and white lady slipper
Mississippi	mockingbird	magnolia	magnolia
Missouri	bluebird	American dogwood	hawthorn
Montana	western meadowlark	Ponderosa pine	bitterroot
Nebraska	western meadowlark	cottonwood	goldenrod
Nevada	mountain bluebird	single-leaf piñon	sagebrush
New Hampshire	purple finch	white birch	purple lilac
New Jersey	eastern goldfinch	red oak	purple violet
New Mexico	roadrunner	piñon pine	yucca
New York	bluebird	sugar maple	rose
North Carolina	cardinal	pine	American dogwood
North Dakota	western meadowlark	American elm	wild prairie rose
Ohio	cardinal	buckeye	scarlet carnation
Oklahoma	scissor-tailed flycatcher	redbud	mistletoe
Oregon	western meadowlark	Douglas fir	Oregon grape
Pennsylvania	ruffled grouse	hemlock	mountain laurel
Rhode Island	Rhode Island red	red maple	violet
South Carolina	Carolina wren	palmetto	Carolina jessamine
South Dakota	ring-necked pheasant	Black Hills spruce	pasque
Tennessee	mockingbird	tulip poplar	iris
Texas	mockingbird	pecan	Texas bluebonnet
Utah	California seagull	blue spruce	sego lily
Vermont	hermit thrush	sugar maple	red clover
Virginia	cardinal	American dogwood	American dogwood
Washington	willow goldfinch	western hemlock	coast rhododendron
West Virginia	cardinal	sugar maple	rhododendron
Wisconsin	robin	sugar maple	wood violet
Wyoming	western meadowlark	cottonwood	Indian paintbrush

HOME PAGE

Hello,

Today we talked about our state bird, tree, and flower. We learned what they looked like and practiced pronouncing their names.

This activity introduces a child to how some things are classified and the differences among these classifications. It also introduces or reinforces geographical boundaries because we discussed how each state has its own official bird, tree, and flower. Lastly, it helps develop within a child a sense of belonging. It is his or her state's bird, tree, and flower.

Our state_____

Bird _____

Tree _____

Flower _____

As you drive throughout your state, look out for the state bird, tree, and flower.

If you travel to different states, be sure to add to your trip by asking your child if he or she knows the bird, tree, and flower of the state you are visiting.

If you discuss where relatives or visitors are from, ask your child questions about your relatives' or visitors' state birds, trees, and flowers.

During your discussions, entertain your child by asking if he or she can find the following:

- five things the same color as his or her state bird, tree, and flower
- five different types of birds, trees, and flowers
- five things special to his or her state or where he or she lives

Have fun!

Name _____

Birds, Trees, and Flowers Practice

Circle all the birds in this picture.

Name _____

Birds, Trees, and Flowers Practice *(cont.)*

Circle all the trees in this picture.

Name _____

Birds, Trees, and Flowers Practice *(cont.)*

Circle all the flowers in this picture.

Continents

WHAT

There are seven main land areas, or *continents*, on Earth. They are Africa, Antarctica, Asia, Australia, Europe, North America, and South America. This lesson introduces the seven continents.

WHY

Preschool children do not understand much of the world's geography. *Oceans, continents, countries,* and *states* are words that have little meaning. Geography often means only their immediate surroundings. Maps, dependent on perspectives and proportions, are meaningless. Despite this, introducing geographical terms and maps into a child's vocabulary sets the stage for further learning. It provides a framework from which children can continue to add information, sort and classify it, and finally gain real understanding. Introducing continents is an engaging way to introduce the basics of geography because it introduces geographical terms and:

- begins to familiarize a child with continent shapes and how they look on maps
- provides a framework for geographical discussions
- provides practice learning and articulating new words
- reinforces basic counting up to seven

HOW

Before starting this lesson, a teacher should find a world map and globe to use as visual aids. A teacher should also have separate maps of the seven continents. Copies of the Continents Practice pages (pages 243–249) will suffice for the continent maps, if desired. In addition, a teacher should make large flashcards printed with the names of the seven continents.

Begin this lesson by showing a globe to the children. Ask them if they know what it is. Explain that it represents Earth, the planet on which we live. Next, ask the children if they can tell which part of the globe is land and which part is water. Point out to the children where they are located on the globe. Next, point to the world map and say, "This is a picture of Earth flattened out. If you were a ship captain or a submarine pilot or just someone driving down the road, it might be a little too much to carry a globe. A flat map is a lot easier. We can put flat maps in books and in pockets." Then, ask the children to find the water and the land on the flat map. Show them where they are located. Ask the children if any of them have ever flown in an airplane or looked down from a high place and seen the land and the water masses from above.

Engage the children in the next part of the lesson by saying, "Today we are going to be learning all about the land. There are special names to use. Do you notice how much of the land is separated by oceans, and how it is spread over the globe? Scientists and geographers have decided that our land is divided into seven main masses, or *continents*. Let's see if we can find one." Lead the children to find Africa, Antarctica, Asia, Australia, Europe, North America, and South America.

Continents *(cont.)*

HOW *(cont.)*

Explain next that they will be learning a few fun things about each continent once they practice counting to seven, since there are seven continents. Have children count to seven several times. If children are at the level where they can count backward, this can be done also. If desired, a teacher can have children jump up, clap, or shout loudly the number *one* since you are going to be working on the first continent.

Display the flashcard for Africa. Have children repeat the word about twenty-five times. The word should not be repeated all at once, but interspersed between finding it on the globe, on the world map, and then being shown the individual continent map. The word can be pronounced in sets of five and spoken quickly, slowly, loudly, and softly. Depending on what other lessons a teacher has covered, a teacher may want to ask about number of syllables and letters, identification of vowels, and what are the beginning and ending sounds and letters of the word.

Engage the children in a conversation where some fun facts are brought up about Africa. One might want to mention the animals found there, the Nile and Congo Rivers, the pyramids in Egypt, and the great Sahara desert. To incorporate physical activity into this lesson, have children roar like a lion, act as if they are hot and need a drink in the desert, hide their heads in the sand like an ostrich, slither like a snake, and run quickly in place as if they were cheetahs. They can also act like an elephant and use their arms as trunks, reaching high above their heads for tree leaves.

It is up to a teacher how many continents to introduce in one day. If the second continent lesson is on the same day or even days later, the procedure will be the same. The teacher should have children practice counting to seven, and this time, children jump up or clap on the number *two*. Next, have children say, "Africa, Antarctica." Have them do this only a few times to review the pronunciation of Africa, and then focus all attention on Antarctica. Bring out the flashcard with the word *Antarctica* printed on it. Repeat all activities done for the word *Africa*. Engage the children in a conversation about some of the fun facts about Antarctica such as how cold it is, how it is covered in snow and ice, that the South Pole is located there, and that penguins live there, as do seals, whales, and special types of seabirds. To incorporate physical activity, one may want to have the children pretend to shiver, walk bent over as if they are being blown by the wind, walk like a penguin, bark like a seal, etc.

Continue with the remaining continents, each time counting and reviewing the names of the continents already taught. Fun facts that might be included for Asia are that panda bears, tigers, and monkeys live there, the Great Wall of China is located there, as well as temples, rice fields, and vast forests and plains in Russia, the high mountains of the Himalayas, etc. To incorporate physical activity while talking about Asia, one might have children act as if they are walking on the Great Wall, eating bamboo like a panda, roaring like a tiger, etc.

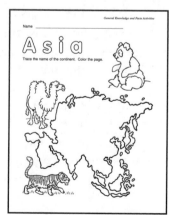

Continents *(cont.)*

HOW *(cont.)*

For Australia, one can mention koala bears, kangaroos, dingoes, and wombats. The dry outback can be mentioned, as well as the Great Barrier Reef. Children can physically act out hopping like a kangaroo, climbing a tree like a koala bear, barking like a dingo, or walking across the hot outback.

For Europe, one can mention the chamois, stork, bear, and reindeer. Mention the great cities of Venice with its canals, the Eiffel Tower in Paris, windmills in the Netherlands, mountains in Switzerland, etc. Physical activities can include pretend mountain climbing, behaving like animals, climbing the Eiffel Tower, moving one's arms like a windmill, etc.

For North America, one can mention animals such as deer, buffalo, elk, moose, caribou, black, brown, grizzly, and polar bears, raccoons, and monkeys (Central America). Physical landmarks can be the Rocky, Appalachian, and Sierra Nevada Mountains, Central American jungles, the great Arctic regions of Canada, etc. Physical activities can include acting like animals, climbing, show-shoeing, driving a dog sled, etc.

For South America, one can mention sloths, panthers, condors, the Amazon jungle, etc. One can have the children move as slowly as they can like a giant sloth, then hop like the colorful poison frogs found throughout the Amazonian jungle, and pretend to paddle canoes down the Amazon River.

HANDS-ON ACTIVITIES

Make copies of the Continents Practice pages (pages 243–249). Have each child trace the name of the continent and color the pages. A teacher may choose to have the children work on only one or two pages at a time. (**Note:** The maps provided are not drawn to scale.)

A teacher may choose to have children find pictures of some of the animals or places mentioned for each continent and make a collage.

If a teacher has access to puzzles of the world or continents, this is a great time to put them out.

CLASS EXTENSIONS

A teacher may choose to make copies of the world and state maps provided in the Address lesson (pages 274–275). Children can color the continents different colors. They can circle the one on which they live.

Bring in an atlas and show children how the various maps in it depict climate and geographical features. Next, show how it is divided into specific sections for each continent. List, if desired, some of the individual countries found on each continent.

Place the separate continent outlines around the world map. Tape string or yarn to each small continent map and then attach the strings from the small maps to the parts of the world map they represent. This will reinforce that the small continent maps represent pieces of the world map.

HOME PAGE

Hello,

Today we talked about the seven main land areas, or *continents,* found on Earth. The continents are Africa, Antarctica, Asia, Australia, Europe, North America, and South America.

Introducing continents is an engaging way to introduce geographical terms and provide a framework for geographical discussions. It familiarizes a child with continent shapes and how they look on maps, as well as provides practice learning and pronouncing new words. It also reviews and reinforces basic counting up to seven.

Engage your child by asking him or her to repeat the names of the seven continents. Or, ask him or her fun questions about continents, such as:

"I see a lion. Could I be in Antarctica or Africa?"

"I start with an 'S.' Am I Australia or South America?"

"You live on this continent. Is it North America or Australia?"

"I see a kangaroo hopping. Am I in Europe or Australia?"

"I see the Eiffel Tower in Paris, France. Am I in South America or Europe?"

"I am floating down the Nile River. Am I in North America or Africa?"

Have fun!

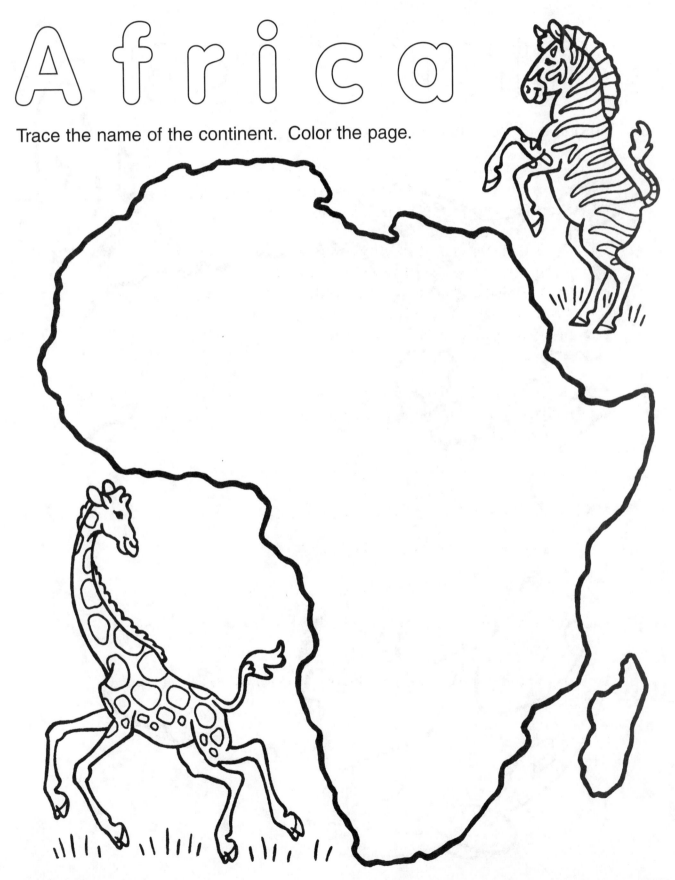

Name _____

Africa

Trace the name of the continent. Color the page.

Name _____

Antarctica

Trace the name of the continent. Color the page.

244   ©Teacher Created Resources, Inc.

Name _____

Asia

Trace the name of the continent. Color the page.

Name _____

Australia

Trace the name of the continent. Color the page.

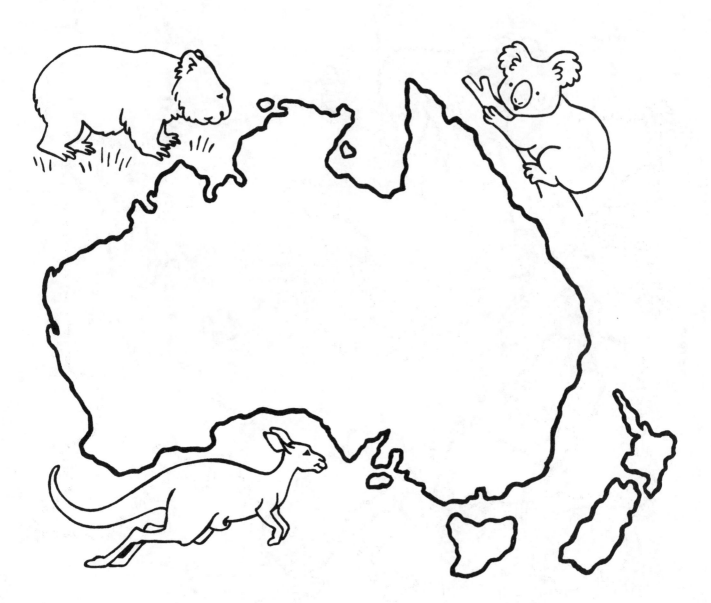

246

Name _____

Europe

Trace the name of the continent. Color the page.

Name _____

North America

Trace the name of the continent. Color the page.

248

Name _____

South America

Trace the name of the continent. Color the page.

Days of the Week

WHAT

There are seven days in each week: Sunday, Monday, Tuesday, Wednesday, Thursday, Friday, and Saturday. This lesson focuses on the days of the week and their sequential order.

WHY

Children's concept of time needs to be developed. They are unclear about the lengths of days, weeks, months, and years. As children are introduced to and become familiar with words such as *days* and *weeks*, they begin to develop a framework of how time fits together.

This particular exercise on the days of the week provides a child practice with:

- pronouncing of the days of the week
- sequencing and ordering skills (Tuesday always follows Monday; Friday always follows Thursday; etc.)
- memorizing facts
- calendar skills—children can look at a calendar and see how it is divided into weeks, with each week having the same number of days
- reading skills—familiarity with the names of the days of the week will be a plus when it comes to children learning how to read them
- anticipating what follows what on a calendar

HOW

Choose a particular physical motion that can be performed safely and easily such as jumping up, stamping one's foot, twirling around, and clapping one's hands. Next, recite the days of the week, Sunday through Saturday, with an emphasis on the first syllable of each day. When the actual day of the week is recited, perform the physical activity.

For example, suppose it is Wednesday and the motion of twirling around has been chosen. Everyone would recite "Sunday, Monday, Tuesday" together. As "Wednesday" is recited, everyone twirls around. Finish with "Thursday, Friday, Saturday."

This activity only takes minutes and can be easily incorporated into circle time or waiting times every day.

As students become familiar with weekday order, a teacher may wish to add to the lesson by printing the days of the week in large letters on a banner or board. Each word can be pointed to as it is recited, or the actual day of the week word can be identified.

Days of the Week *(cont.)*

HANDS-ON PRACTICE

Make copies of the days of the week cards (pages 253–255) for each student. Engage students in a coloring activity where they trace over the letters on the cards. As the class recites the days, children can lay out their cards in the correct order. (A teacher may want to have the words listed on a bulletin board in sequential order for easy reference during this activity so that children can complete this task by matching rather than by reading.)

After the cards are in sequential order, a teacher can ask the students to identify the present day of the week and have them pick up or touch the card. Teachers can also have students match their cards to a real calendar, naming the days as they pair them.

CLASS EXTENSIONS

When a group of students reaches a level where they can easily recite the days of the week, one can alter the starting day from Sunday to the actual day of the week. For example, on a Tuesday, recite "Tuesday, Wednesday, Thursday," and so on, instead of starting with Sunday. This exercise reinforces that time has sequential rules—a Wednesday always follows a Tuesday, etc.

Have children look at a calendar and see how the number date corresponds to a weekday.

Have children look on a daily newspaper for the printed date.

If one wants to incorporate math, one can start having children count how many days "until." For example, "Today is Monday. We will go on a field trip on Thursday. We have Tuesday, Wednesday, and then Thursday. How many days until Thursday?" (When this type of questioning begins, a teacher might want to have students lay out their flash cards in sequential order or refer to a class calendar so they have a visual aid.)

HOME PAGE

Hello,

Today we recited the days of the week in sequential order. Each time a particular day came up, we engaged in a physical activity like jumping up or clapping our hands.

A young child's concept of time needs to be developed, so we will repeat this activity quite often over the year.

This particular activity provides practice with the pronunciation of the names of the days of the week, sequencing and ordering skills, memorizing, calendar skills, and reading skills.

Reciting the days of the week can be used to engage your child while he or she is a passenger in a car or any other time one thinks about it.

If you have a family calendar, show your child where the weekday is marked.

Use the daily newspaper to show your child where the date is printed. Ask him or her to read it. Direct him or her by asking, "Yesterday was Monday. What do you think this day is right here?" "Yes, today is Tuesday. So what day do you think the newspaper will print here tomorrow?"

Have fun!

Days of the Week Practice

Trace or color the names of the days of the week. Cut out the cards and paste them in order on a large sheet of paper.

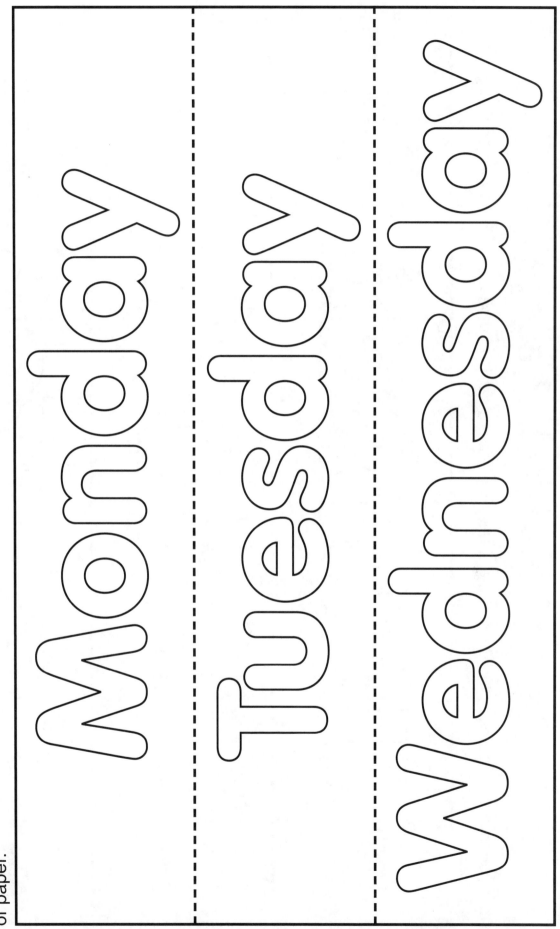

Days of the Week Practice *(cont.)*

Trace or color the names of the days of the week. Cut out the cards and paste them in order on a large sheet of paper.

Thursday

Friday

Saturday

Days of the Week Practice *(cont.)*

Trace or color the names of the days of the week. Cut out the cards and paste them in order on a large sheet of paper.

Months of the Year

WHAT

Our calendar year is divided into twelve *months*: January, February, March, April, May, June, July, August, September, October, November, and December. This lesson focuses on the names of the twelve months of the year and their sequential order.

WHY

Children are expected to know in which month they were born, in which month certain holidays fall, and the current date. Time, and how it passes, is a concept that children are not born knowing. It needs to be developed.

Practicing month order can help a child understand that time is not random. Its passage is orderly and ruled. This particular exercise on month order provides a child practice with:

- pronunciation of month names
- month sequence
- where rites of passage, such as birthdays and holidays, fit into the month sequence
- anticipating, listening for, and remaining still until the appropriate physical response is required

HOW

The first step is for the teacher to name the months in order, aloud: January, February, March, April, May, June, July, August, September, October, November, and December.

There should not be pauses between the names, and the words should be spoken in a singsong manner. One may choose to stress the beginning of each month by a tilt of the head or clapping.

Some teachers may choose to print the names of the months on a board and point to each name as it is spoken or laminate a set of student flash cards (pages 259–262).

Ask children to repeat the months with you. Do not worry if children cannot keep up in the beginning. As this exercise is repeated over time, students will gain mastery.

The second step involves incorporating the date. Typically, this can be done after one basic repetition.   Ask the children or explain which month it is. Then, while reciting the months, have the children shout, whisper, and/or squat down, and then jump up when they come to the appropriate month in the sequence. The key is not to stop at the designated month, but to keep on with the entire sequence. The physical activity is done only during the time the designated month is named.

Months of the Year *(cont.)*

HOW *(cont.)*

The third step focuses on individual class interest and rites of passage. Perhaps one child can pick a holiday or someone's birthday. The entire class shouts, whispers, or jumps up during the recitation on the month in which the particular holiday or event falls.

This activity only takes minutes and can be easily incorporated into circle time. As a general rule of thumb, it should not be repeated more than three times a day.

HANDS-ON PRACTICE

Make copies of the Months of the Year cards (pages 259–262) for each child. Have students trace or color their sets of cards. Students can use special markings or designs on appropriate cards to designate birthdays or holidays. As a teacher reads the names of the months to the students, the students can place the months in order by pasting them to a board or lining them up.

CLASS EXTENSIONS

When a group of students reaches a level where they can easily recite the months, as well as respond physically to the present or designated month, one can alter the starting month. If it is November, for example, one can recite "November, December, January" and so on, instead of starting the recitation with January. This exercise allows children to practice starting in the middle and reinforces the notion that certain months always follow other months.

One can also extend this activity to incorporate beginning sounds. A teacher might state, "Let's jump up on the month that begins with the letter 's.' What does the 's' sound like? Is there a month that begins with that sound? Let's jump up on September, the month that begins with the letter 's.'"

A teacher may also extend this activity by grouping months by seasons. He or she can engage the children in a conversation where children decide if a month like January, for example, would be included in a list of months for fall, winter, spring, or summer.

HOME PAGE

Hello,

Today we practiced saying the months of the year by reciting them in order, and then jumping or clapping on a designated month.

This activity helps a child practice pronouncing month names, familiarizes a child with month sequence, and helps a child begin to understand where rites of passage, such as birthdays and holidays, fit into the month sequence. Lastly, it allows a child to anticipate, listen for, and practice holding one's self still until the appropriate physical response is required.

Reciting the months in order is an activity that can take place while your child is a passenger in a car. Have him or her shout, whisper, or clap on a specific month. Personalize it by having your child respond on the months in which different family members were born, his or her favorite month, when he or she might see snow, when he or she might go swimming, etc.

Have fun!

Months of the Year Practice

Color or trace the names of the months. Cut them out and paste them in order on a large sheet of paper.

January

Febuary

March

Months of the Year Practice (cont.)

Color or trace the names of the months. Cut them out and paste them in order on a large sheet of paper.

April

May

June

Months of the Year Practice *(cont.)*

Color or trace the names of the months. Cut them out and paste them in order on a large sheet of paper.

July

August

September

Months of the Year Practice *(cont.)*

Color or trace the names of the months. Cut them out and paste them in order on a large sheet of paper.

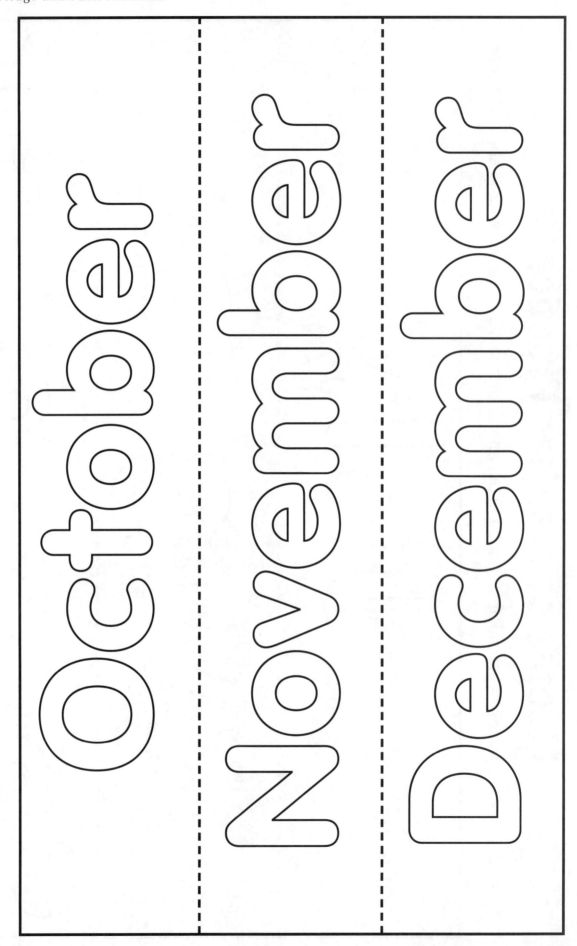

Phone Numbers

WHAT

Businesses, families, and individuals all use phones and each phone has a unique phone number. This lesson focuses on teaching each child his or her home phone number.

WHY

As children begin to gain independence, they need to know basic information about themselves. One's phone number is an important bit of information. Teaching a child his or her phone number provides:

- number recognition practice
- practice memorizing numbers in sequence
- awareness of communication networks
- an avenue to discuss proper phone usage
- an avenue to practice how to respond when talking on a phone

HOW

In preparation for this lesson, a teacher should have ready a list of all of the students' primary phone numbers. The numbers should be easy to read and printed on strips of paper. Each child will be given his or her own number later during the lesson.

Also, a teacher may want to bring in a phone as a visual prompt, or he or she can use a copy of the Phone Number Practice page (page 267).

Begin by asking children how they talk to each other. Next, ask them how they can communicate with people far away. Once the word *telephone* comes up, ask for some situations in which a telephone could be used. Some sample situations are:

- you call to ask someone to come over
- you call a doctor or 911 if you are hurt
- you want to order food
- you want to find out how someone is doing, feeling, etc.
- you are a newspaper reporter, and you want to report what has happened and what you have seen
- you want to find out if a store has a certain item or what time a movie plays

Next, ask children how they know which number to call. What gets the phone to ring at the proper place—at your friend's house rather than the school?

At this point, bring up the notion of individual phone numbers. Each house phone has a different number, and each cell phone has a different number. Explain that they are going to be working on memorizing individual phone numbers. Hold up a printed phone number (perhaps the school's) and ask the children to observe how it is written.

Have children count the number of digits. Explain that studies have shown that people can memorize seven digits without too much work. Explain that phone numbers are easier to memorize because they are broken into "chunks," or pieces. The first chunk has three numbers, and the second chunk has four numbers.

Phone Numbers *(cont.)*

HOW *(cont.)*

Hand each child his or her printed number. Together as a class, count up to seven quickly as every child counts the number of digits. Next, ask children to focus on the first three numbers. Have them say these three digits over several times—five times loudly, five times slowly, five times quickly, five times with their eyes closed, etc. Then have them write the digits in the air (if they are familiar with numbers) and on the palms of their hands with their fingers.

Engage children in a question session where you ask, "How many people have a one (two, three, etc.) as their first (second, third) number?"

Before moving on to work with the next digits, caution children that memorizing a phone number often takes several days of practice. This is their first day, and they will find that when they do this again it will be easier.

Have children look at the fourth and fifth digits. Have them repeat these two digits several times. Then, have them add these digits onto the first three. Have children repeat the same exercises you did with just the first three—saying them five times fast, loudly, softly, slowly, with their eyes closed, etc. Then have them write all five digits in the air and on the palms of their hands with their fingers.

Repeat with the last two digits.

Next, play a Detective Game where you have children stand with their phone number cards in front of them. Say, "If I were going to call XXX–XXXX, would I be calling _____ or _____?"

Another game that a teacher can play is one that incorporates how to answer a phone. First, ask children how they know who it is on the other end of the line. Explain that often it is hard to tell, so to help the person you are calling, you should always identify yourself. Practice saying,

"Hello, this is _____. How may I help you?"

"Hello, this is _____. May I please talk to _____?"

Next, the teacher can say, "Number XXX–XXXX, you are calling XXX-XXXX. Ask him or her if you can go out to play." The entire class can make a ringing sound, and then listen while the children with the designated phone numbers speak.

"Hello, this is _____. How may I help you?"

"Hello _____. This is _____. I wanted to know if you could come out to play."

Teacher Note: Each family has different rules about identifying themselves when answering the telephone. For safety reasons, some prefer not to identify themselves unless the person calling is known to them. Practice a variety of methods with students and discuss reasons for each.

Phone Numbers *(cont.)*

HANDS-ON PRACTICE

Make phone number strips for each child. Write the name and phone number of each student on the strip. Additional copies can be made for children to copy and practice writing their own names and numbers after the lesson for hands-on practice.

Make copies for each child of the Phone Number Practice pages (pages 267–269). On the practice pages with the seven telephones, teachers should instruct students to write their phone numbers at the bottom of the pages on the blanks provided. Then, using those numbers as a reference, have children color the matching numbers on the phones above the blanks or paste a matching number of small counters (such as beans, buttons, pieces of paper, etc.) on the phones above the blanks.

A teacher may also have his or her students make three-dimensional models of their phone numbers by lining up seven piles of blocks, with the number of blocks in the first pile corresponding to the first digit of their telephone number, the number of blocks in the second pile corresponding to the second digit of their telephone number, and so on.

If a teacher desires, he or she can have children make their three-dimensional model with small tongue depressors, lining up the stacks on a large sheet of paper and pasting them in place.

CLASS EXTENSIONS

Have children practice dialing numbers with real phones. Have children call from one cell phone to another. They can simply call each other from across the room, or with one child standing outside. If a pay phone is nearby, one can have children call from the pay phone or to the pay phone.

Remind children to identify themselves on the phone—otherwise the person on the other line might not know who they are.

At some point, children may ask if it is possible to have the same phone number as someone else. A teacher can respond to this question by bringing up country codes, area codes, and prefixes. Bring in a phone book and open it up to the page where area codes are shown on a map. Explain how the same numbers can be used as long as they have different area codes, as each area code covers a distinct and different part of the country.

Use the same phone book to show children how numbers are listed by city and in alphabetical order.

Ask children to pick a country on the map. Then, find the page in the phone book that lists foreign country codes. Show children the codes for the country, and then say, "Once we have the country, we still have to know the area code and the phone number."

HOME PAGE

Hello,

Today we talked about phone numbers. The children began to memorize their own phone numbers.

This activity introduces a child to communication methods. It also helps a child practice memorizing numbers in sequence.

Help your child memorize his or her phone number with some simple activities.

Every time you get in the car or need to pass time while waiting, have your child recite your phone number three times. The first time, you will need to recite the number with your child.

Play Yes-and-No games with your phone number. Call out made-up phone numbers intermixed with your actual phone number. The child must answer yes or no, depending on whether or not it is your phone number.

When we practiced talking on the phone, we used these forms of greeting when answering the phone or placing a call.

   "Hello, this is _____. How may I help you?"

   "Hello, this is _____. May I please talk to _____?"

Have fun!

Name _____

Phone Numbers Practice

Color these telephones. Circle what type of phone you have in your house.

Phone Numbers Practice *(cont.)*

Color the number on each phone that matches the digits of your telephone number.

Name _____

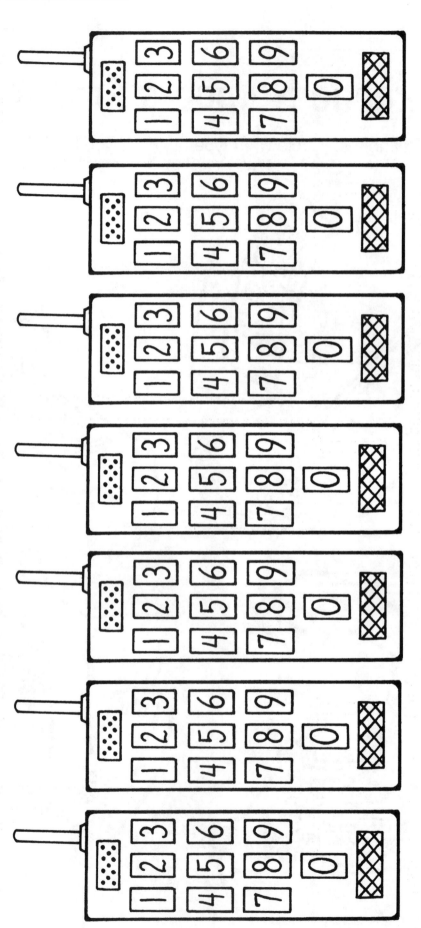

Write your number above.

Phone Numbers Practice (cont.)

Name _____

Paste or draw items that match the digits of your telephone number on each phone.

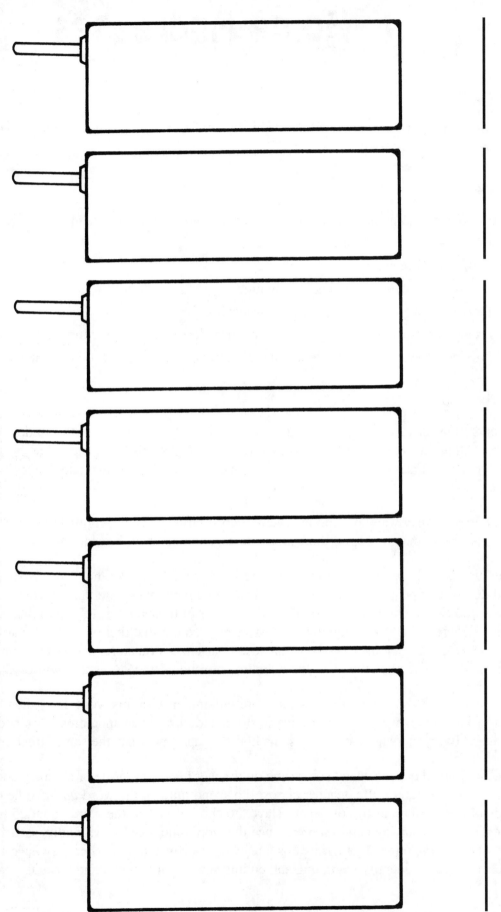

Write your number above.

Home Addresses

WHAT

An *address* designates where one lives. This lesson focuses on teaching each child his or her home address.

WHY

Being able to tell someone where one lives is considered a life skill. Helping a child memorize his or her address can:

- reinforce a life skill
- provide practice memorizing information
- familiarize a child with the concept of location
- provide an introduction to geographical terms like street, state, country, and continent
- provide an avenue for introducing a child to maps (See the unit on continents, page 239.)

HOW

In preparation for this lesson, a teacher should have ready a list of all of the students' addresses. The numbers should be easy to read and printed on individual strips of paper. A teacher may choose to laminate them. Each child will be given the paper with his or her own address on it later during the lesson.

Also, a teacher may want to bring in several maps to use as visual prompts. He or she should have a city map, a state map, a map of the United States, and one of the world.

Begin the lesson by asking children to picture in their minds where they live. Next, ask them how they could describe to people where they live. How could they make sure that someone could find the way to their homes? If children mention the size or color of their homes, tell them that while they are correct and are doing good thinking, it must be pointed out that there are lots of particular sized and colored homes. If they mention that it is close to a school or a store, point out again that while they are right and doing excellent thinking, there are lots of schools and stores that houses can be next to.

Bring up the word *address*. If the children are unfamiliar with this word, have them repeat it several times. Explain that every person, business, store, and library has an address. An address tells where one lives. Everyone who lives in the same house or apartment has the same street or building address.

A teacher may choose to spend some time on the word *address*, or he or she may choose to focus only on the address location. If a teacher chooses to spend time on the word *address*, he or she should have a copy of the word on a strip of paper. Have the children repeat the word about 25 times, breaking up the repetitions by having children pronounce the word quickly, slowly, loudly, softly, and in a silly voice. Depending on what other lessons a teacher has covered, a teacher may have children count vowels and letters, identify beginning and ending sounds and letters, and write the word in the air.

Home Addresses *(cont.)*

HOW *(cont.)*

Next, point to the world map. Explain that everything in the world is on the planet Earth. Earth is a big place, and so we have to narrow it down or be more precise when we tell someone where we live if we want him or her to be able to find us. Point out the continents, emphasizing the continent on which they live. Next, bring it down to the country level. Go on to the state level and city level. For the state level, bring out a map of the United States, and for the city level, bring out a state map and show where the city is located on it. At each level, have the children repeat fives times each the names of the planet, continent, country, state, country, and city loudly, very softly, with their eyes closed, and as fast as they can.

At this point, hand each a copy of his or her printed address. Ask him or her to compare the address to a child's sitting next to him or her. Are some things the same? Are some things different?

Next, explain that just as children learn their names, they can learn their addresses. Read the children their street names. Have children repeat their street names five times for each activity while speaking loudly, softly, with their eyes closed, as fast as they can, and while jumping. If some children live on the same street, make sure that it is pointed out.

Bring out a city map and show children how streets are marked on the map. If a teacher has time, he or she might put pins in the map marking the streets on which the children live.

Next, ask children, "Okay, now we are on the right street. How do we get them to your exact house or building?"

At this point, have children look at their address pages again. Ask them if they have any numbers on the pages. Explain that this number allows the mail deliverer and the fire department and any other visitor to know exactly where one lives on the street. Have children read the numbers aloud.

Inform the children that it takes a lot of time to learn an address, so for today, they are just going to practice saying the numbers. It will get easier to say and to remember after they do this for several days.

A teacher may decide to only work on one or two numbers at a time. Have children say the numbers several times while engaging in different activities (speaking as fast as they can, speaking loudly or softly, and picturing the numbers in front of them with their eyes closed.)

Finally, engage children in a question-and-answer game where they have to respond to the teacher's questions. Sample questions might be:

"Do we live on the planet Earth or the planet Mercury?"

"Do we live on the continent of North America or South America?"

"Do we live in the state of California or New York?"

"Do we live in the city of Lafayette or San Francisco?"

"Does _____ (child in class) live on _____ Street or _____ Street?"
(Name two streets on which children in the class live.)

Home Addresses *(cont.)*

HOW *(cont.)*

"Does _____ (child in class) live at _____ or _____?" (Say two different addresses of children in class.)

"If I tell someone that I live in Texas, is that enough for them to figure out where I live?"

"If I tell someone I live at 269, is that enough for them to figure out where I live?"

HANDS-ON PRACTICE

Have each child paste the numbers of his or her address onto a piece of paper. The children can use the same page used during the lesson with his or her address printed on it as a reference. Numbers can be copied from the number cards (pages 179–185) or cut from colored paper. Have children draw pictures of their houses on the pieces of paper.

If there is wall space, the city map can be hung on the wall. The decorated and pasted address papers can be hung around the map, with yarn strings leading to pins placed on the map where they live.

Have children color the part of the world map (page 274) and/or United States map (page 275) where they live.

CLASS EXTENSIONS

Have children bring a piece of mail from home. Have them each find their address on the envelope.

If funds allow, a teacher may buy a postcard and address it for each child. The child then has to find the postcard with his or her address and decorate it. The teacher should mail all the cards on the same day. Then, the child can count the number of days it takes for the postcard to be delivered to his or her house.

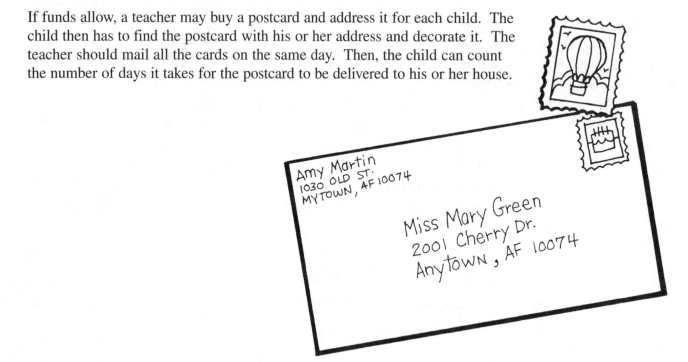

HOME PAGE

Hello,

Today we talked about addresses. We started with our planet Earth, and then went to our continent, country, state, county, city, and street. We started memorizing our street addresses.

Discussing addresses enables a child to practice memorizing information. It introduces a child to geographical terms and the purpose of maps. It familiarizes a child with the concept of location.

Help your child memorize his or her address by having him or her recite it three times every time you get in a car or are waiting for time to pass. When you first begin this activity, your child will need to recite the address with you. As time goes on, your child will remember more and more on his or her own.

Your child will also enjoy answering questions about where he or she lives.

Here are some sample questions:

"Do you live on the planet Earth or the planet Neptune?"

"Do you live on the continent of Australia or the continent of North America?"

"Do you live in the United States or in Canada?"

"Do you live in the state of Arizona or Utah?"

"Do you live in the city of San Jose or Crawfordsville?"

"Do you live on Elm Street or Cherry Street?"

"Do you live at _____ (your correct number) or 725?"

Have fun!

Name _____

Addresses Practice

Find what continent you live in on the map of the world. Color it.

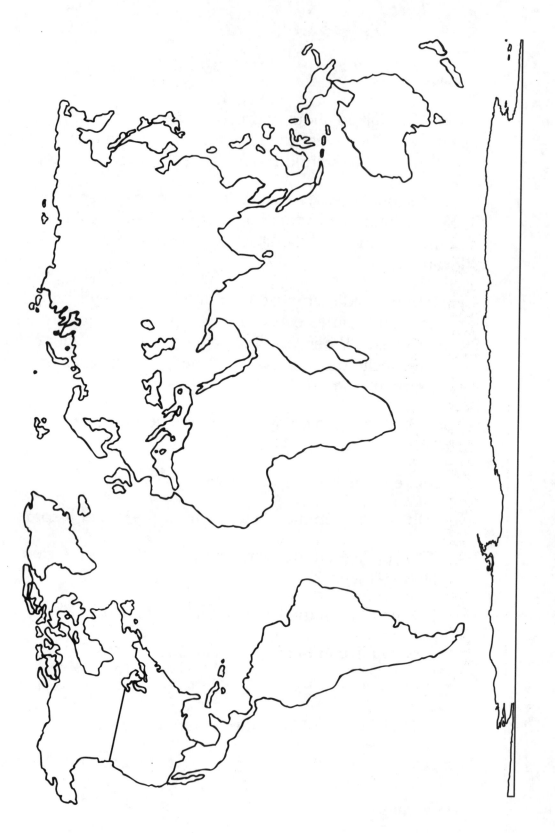

Name _____

Home Addresses Practice *(cont.)*

Find what state you live in on the United States map. Color it.

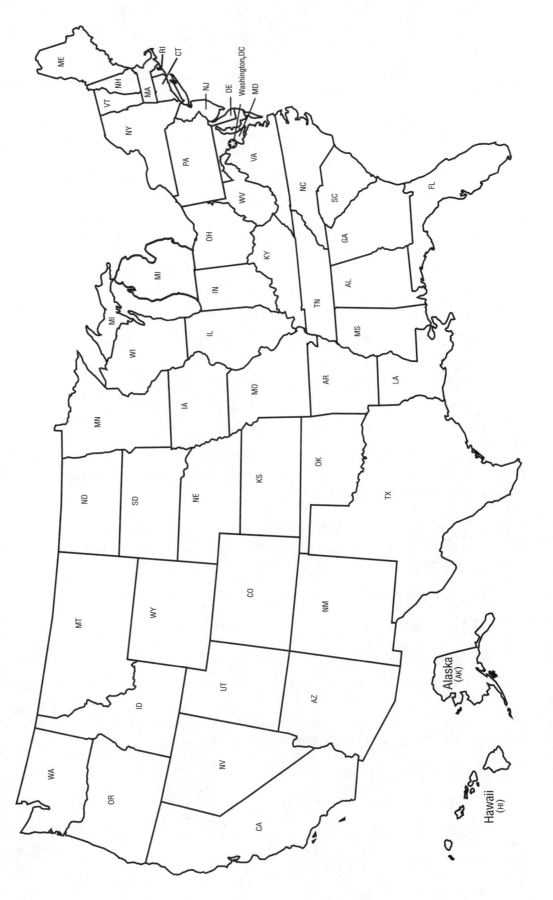

True or False

WHAT

We are supposed to know the difference between what is true and what is false. We are often asked to judge or decide if something is true or false. Decisions about true and false are developmental.

Children need to develop the concept of truth. This lesson focuses on making decisions about what can be true and what can be false.

WHY

Children learn what is true and what is not by experience. They sort through information they see, hear, feel, and sense. Engaging children in activities where they decide if something is true or false:

- teaches the meaning of the words *true* and *false*
- provides a child practice with decision making
- develops reasoning skills
- familiarizes a child with a common test question form

HOW

A teacher may want to print the words *true* and *false* on large cards and laminate them as visual prompts for this lesson. Or, he or she may use True or False Practice (page 279). The teacher will hold up or point to the appropriate word during the lesson.

First, bring up the word *true* in discussion. Ask children if they know what it means. Lead them into agreeing that when something is true, it cannot be false. It is real. It is what happened. Reinforce the meaning with examples.

"Is it true that today is _____ ?" (appropriate day)

"Is it true that _____ is wearing _____ ?"

"Is it true that my hair is _____ ?"

"Is it true that a dog has two eyes?"

Next, bring up the opposite of true. If something is not true, it is *false*. It is not real. It is not genuine. It is not right. Reinforce the meaning with examples.

"Is it true that the ceiling is on the floor?"

"Is it true that a dog has five tails?"

"Is it true that a cat can fly?"

"Is it true that _____ has _____ hair?"

True or False *(cont.)*

HOW *(cont.)*

Follow this with an exercise in which you have children respond by answering true or false. Mix silly statements in with more concrete ones for entertaining purposes. The following are some sample statements.

_____ is bigger than a car.

_____ came to school today in an airplane.

_____ is four years old.

_____ is 54 years old!

Apples are red.

Apples are green.

Apples are purple with yellow stripes.

There is a spider on my neck.

I am wearing shoes today.

HANDS-ON PRACTICE

Make enough copies of the words *true* and *false* from the True or False Practice page (page 279) for each child. Have the children trace the letters on each word. Suggest making each word a different color. Have the children raise the appropriate card in response to the questions asked.

CLASS EXTENSION

Extend this type of question to books that are being read in class. Preface the questions now with the words, "In the book, _____?" If, for example, the book *The Cat in the Hat* has been read in class, you could use these sample statements:

"In the book, the cat wore a hat."

"In the book, the cat wore a broom."

"In the book, there were Things One, Two, and Three."

"In the book, a fish was worried about trouble."

"In the book, the cat went to the doctor."

Note that this type of questioning encourages active listening. It helps a child recall facts and details about what he or she has heard.

Some teachers may choose to have children have their true and false cards with them while a book is being read or even if a class exercise is going on. Then, he or she can have the children incorporate physical activity (holding up the cards) during the question-and-answer period after the activity.

HOME PAGE

Hello,

Today we discussed the words *true* and *false*. We came up with lots of examples of what could be true and what could be false.

A child learns what is true and what is not by experience. He or she sorts through information seen, heard, felt, and sensed. Engaging your child in activities where he or she decides if something is true or false provides a child with practice making decisions and develops reasoning skills. It familiarizes a child with a common form of test question.

Giving your child true and false statements is an entertaining time-filler while driving in a car or waiting in line.

These are some sample statements:

"Your name is _____." (true or false)

"You have three eyes." (true or false)

"There is a white car behind us." (true or false)

"There is a cat in the yard." (true or false)

"In the story 'Jack and the Beanstalk,' Jack planted corn." (true or false)

"We live in _____." (true or false)

Have fun!

True or False Practice

Trace or color these words. Cut out the cards. Hold up the **true** word when something is true. Hold up the **false** word when something is false.

Opposites

WHAT

An *antonym* is a word that is opposite in meaning to another word. The opposite of *hot* is *cold*. The opposite of *big* is *small*. This lesson focuses on words and their antonyms.

WHY

Children will be tested on vocabulary in a variety of ways throughout their academic years. Often, finding word opposites or antonyms will be included in test formats. Introducing word opposites does more than increase a child's vocabulary. It also helps a child understand how individual words relate to each other. Being able to come up with a word's opposite demonstrates an understanding of word meanings. Activities with word opposites:

- build vocabulary
- build word relationships
- develop reasoning skills

HOW

Introduce the idea of word opposites by engaging children in a question-and-answer exercise. Using the antonym pair *hot—cold* as an example, one would first ask the children, "Are you hot?" Lead them to the word *cold* by asking, "If you weren't hot, what would you be?" A teacher may have to lead children to the word *cold* by asking questions such as, "If you weren't hot, would you be cold or would you be a kitten?"

Once the children have spoken the words *hot* and *cold*, have the children repeat the pair. Explain that *hot* and *cold* are word opposites.

Immediately offer another example and ask children if they can come up with its opposite. "The opposite of *go* is . . . ." (*stop*) "The opposite of *full* is . . . ." (*empty*). To ensure success with these introductory pairs, a teacher may need to lead children to the correct answers. For example, he or she might say, "Could the opposite of *go* be *hamburger* or *stop*?" "Could the opposite of *big* be *small* or *table*?"

Continue this type of dialogue with children until they become familiar with the idea of word opposites. Note that even if children reach a level where they can come up with word opposites on their own, they will still enjoy questions with obvious and silly answers, as above.

Reinforce opposite pairs by reversing the word order in the questions. For example, first ask, "What is the opposite of *fast*?" Follow this with, "So the opposite of *fast* is *slow*. What do you think the opposite of *slow* is?"

280

Opposites *(cont.)*

HANDS-ON PRACTICE

Have children act out opposites. For example, have them act as if they are happy. Then instruct them to act out *happy—sad*. Opposites that are easy to act out are *happy—sad; hot—cold; asleep—awake; stand up—lie down; smile—frown; big (stretch out)—small (curl up); noisy—quiet.*

Make copies for each child of the Opposites Practice picture cards (pages 283–287). Have children cut out the cards. Then, the children can match the pictures to the opposites.

Make copies for each child of the last sheet of the Opposites Practice page (page 288). Have children draw lines from the pictures on the top line to pictures on the bottom line, matching opposites.

CLASS EXTENSION

Reinforce word opposites throughout the year by asking children antonym questions with a twist:

"When we go swimming, are we the opposite of cold or big?" (*We are hot when we go swimming so we are the opposite of cold*.)

"My taco is frozen! There is ice on it! It is not hot. It is the opposite of hot. It is _____." (*cold*)

"A tortoise is walking across a field. Is the tortoise slow, or is the tortoise the opposite of slow?" (*slow*)

"I saw a fire truck. Is a fire truck small or the opposite of small?" (*A fire truck is big, the opposite of small.*)

"I just ate the biggest sandwich in the world. Am I full or the opposite of full?" (*full*)

"Everyone is yelling and clapping their hands. Is the classroom quiet or the opposite of quiet?" (*The opposite of quiet—noisy.*)

Common Opposites

high—low	up—down	empty—full	open—close
good—bad	winter—summer	hungry—full	wet—dry
hot—cold	dark—light	easy—hard	stand up—lie down
young—old	asleep—awake	front—back	hard—soft
sick—well	top—bottom	start—finish	heavy—light
fast—slow	stop—go	first—last	happy—sad
big—small	yes—no	quiet—noisy	day—night
sweet—sour	smile—frown	near—far	strong—weak

HOME PAGE

Hello,

Today we talked about words and their opposites (antonyms). The opposite of *hot* is *cold*. The opposite of *big* is *small*.

Introducing word opposites does more than increase a child's vocabulary. It also helps a child understand how individual words relate to each other.

Asking your child questions about opposites is a great way to entertain him or her when he or she is a passenger in a car or waiting in line. Questions can be basic or with a personal twist.

"The opposite of *cold* is . . . ." *(hot)*

"The opposite of *big* is . . . ." *(small)*

"When we jump into a pool, do we get dry or the opposite of dry?" *(the opposite of dry: wet)*

"When something weighs so much that we cannot lift it, is it heavy or the opposite of heavy?" *(heavy)*

"When something weighs so little that it floats away, is it heavy or the opposite of heavy?" *(the opposite of heavy: light)*

Have fun!

Opposites Practice

Color and cut out the cards. Match each card to its opposite. Paste the opposites next to each other on a sheet of paper.

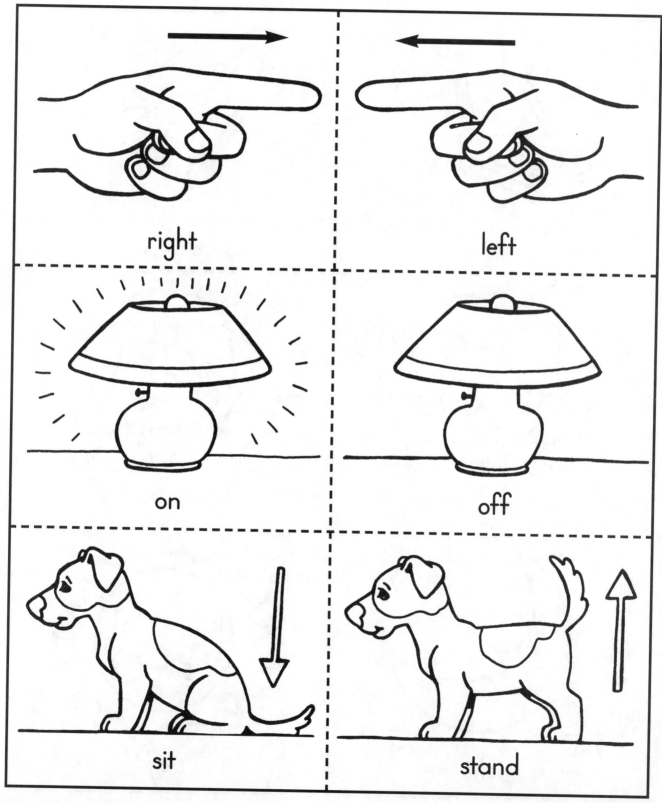

right

left

on

off

sit

stand

Opposites Practice *(cont.)*

Color and cut out the cards. Match each card to its opposite. Paste the opposites next to each other on a sheet of paper.

up

down

boy

girl

night

day

Opposites Practice *(cont.)*

Color and cut out the cards. Match each card to its opposite. Paste the opposites next to each other on a sheet of paper.

laugh

cry

old

new

open

closed

Opposites Practice (cont.)

Color and cut out the cards. Match each card to its opposite. Paste the opposites next to each other on a sheet of paper.

awake

asleep

front

back

in

out

286

Opposites Practice *(cont.)*

Color and cut out the cards. Match each card to its opposite. Paste the opposites next to each other on a sheet of paper.

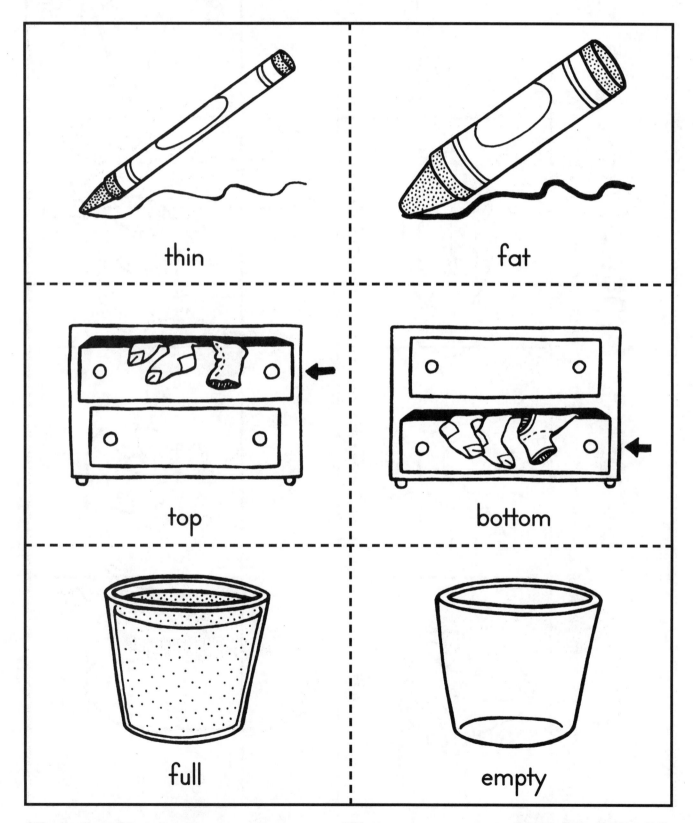

thin

fat

top

bottom

full

empty

Opposites Practice *(cont.)*

Name _____

Draw a line from each picture on the top row to its opposite on the bottom row.

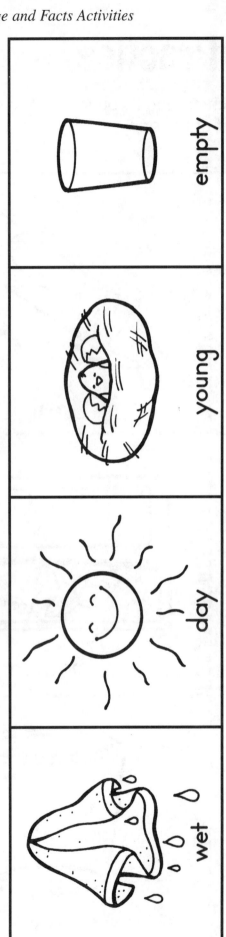

empty

young

day

wet

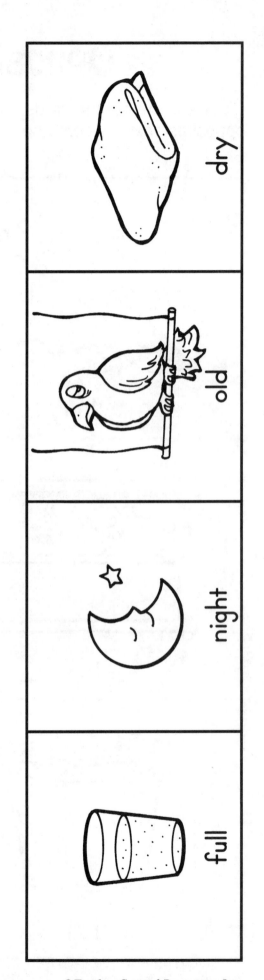

dry

old

night

full

Before and After

WHAT

As children grow, they understand the concept of time. They begin to understand that there is a sequence to events. This lesson focuses on how some things occur *before* others and how some things occur *after* others.

WHY

Having children go through stories and situations where they have to sequence events, decide what comes first, and figure out what comes before and what comes after, helps develop a child's:

- understanding of sequential (first vs. second) order
- understanding of how *before* and *after* relate to each other
- reasoning skills when it comes to deducing sequence in a chain of events

HOW

Engage children in a discussion where you present a situation. "I get an apple. I eat the apple." Ask the children what came first—getting the apple or eating the apple.

Bring up the words *before* and *after*. Explain, "I had to get the apple before I could eat it. After I got the apple, I could eat it." Don't worry if the children seem confused with the words *before* and *after* at first. They will begin to pick it up as more examples are provided. Present more situations, such as,

"I was so sleepy. I went to bed."

"The sun rose in the morning. It set at night."

"There was a puppy. It grew into a big dog."

With each situation, explain that something came first. Something came before something else.

"I was sleepy before I went to bed. I went to bed after I was sleepy."

"The sun rose in the morning before it set at night. It set at night after it rose in the morning."

"There was a puppy before there was a big dog. The puppy grew into a big dog after it was a puppy."

Now, tell the children that they are Before and After Detectives. They have to figure out what came before, and what came after. A teacher might use the following situations, or any others that he or she finds appropriate:

"I light a match. I light a candle."   "I get on my bike. I ride my bike."

"I make a sandwich. I eat the sandwich."   "I plant a seed. A plant grows."

After each example is discussed and children decide what comes before and after, a teacher should reinforce the concepts of before and after by incorporating them into a sentence with the examples. For example, a teacher should respond with something like,

"Yes, I had to light the match before I could light the candle. I lit the candle after I lit the match."

"Yes, I had to make a sandwich before I could eat it. I ate the sandwich after I made it."

"Yes, I had to get on my bike before I could ride it. I rode my bike after I had gotten on."

"Yes, I had to plant the seed before it could grow into a plant. The plant grew after I planted the seed."

Before and After *(cont.)*

HOW *(cont.)*

Now inform the children that the challenge has started! You are going to present things in a mixed-up order. They are going to have to sort out what came first and what came second. Respond to their answers in the same manner as before, always putting the words *before* and *after* into your answers. A teacher might use these situations, or any others that he or she finds appropriate.

- an empty cup; drinking from a cup
- a cup full of milk; milk spilled on the floor
- a plant; planting a seed in the ground
- putting on your shoes; putting on your socks
- running; getting out of breath
- swimming; getting wet
- being really full; eating
- washing your hands; having clean hands
- cutting your hair; having short hair
- the rain stops; the sun comes out
- got sick; ate a hundred worms
- ate candy; brushed teeth
- hurt foot; climbed a hundred flights of stairs

"I had to drink from the cup before it was empty. After I drank, the cup was empty."

"The cup was full of milk before I spilled it. After I filled it, I spilled it."

"I planted a seed in the ground before there was a plant. The seed grew into a plant after it was planted."

HANDS-ON PRACTICE

Make copies for each child of the Before and After Practice pages (pages 292–293). Have children color the cards and then paste them onto a piece of paper or line them up in the correct order.

CLASS EXTENSIONS

Take the same cards (pages 292–293) and have the children write the numbers 1 and 2 on them to indicate before and after.

Have children germinate seeds in class. This can be done by wrapping the seeds in a damp paper towel, placing them in a plastic baggy, and hanging the bags from a clothesline. Have children describe what happened before and what happened after.

HOME PAGE

Hello,

Today we talked about the words *before* and *after*. We put two events in order. We decided which one came first and which one came after.

This activity helps your child gain an understanding of sequence. As your child figures out what has to come before and after, he or she develops reasoning skills.

Engage your child in a Before and After Detective game by giving two situations, and asking him or her to figure out what came first. These are some examples:

- say the names of two family members. Which one came before the other? Which one came after?
- a bowl filled with cereal and milk; a bowl of cereal with just some milk on the bottom
- a bird flying; a baby bird
- children getting in a car; children getting out of a car
- clean teeth; brushing teeth

Have fun!

Before and After Practice

Color and cut out the pictures. Paste them in the order of **before** and **after**.

Before and After Practice *(cont.)*

Color and cut out the pictures. Paste them in the order of **before** and **after**.

Colors

WHAT

The *primary* colors are red, blue, and yellow. *Secondary* colors are made from mixtures of the primary colors. Purple is red and blue. Orange is red and yellow. Green is blue and yellow. This lesson focuses on primary colors and how they can be mixed together to make secondary colors.

WHY

Children are expected to be able to identify and name colors. Typically, we teach color identification through repetition. We show different objects or cards of varying colors and state the color. We expect children to repeat our observations. We do not mention how secondary colors are made until children are older. Preschool children are at an age where they are discovering how things are put together. Introducing the idea of primary and secondary colors while teaching color names:

- introduces the concept that different ingredients make different end products
- helps with color identification
- provides fine motor practice blending and mixing

HOW

A teacher may want to have colored blocks or laminated color strips to use as visual prompts for this exercise.

Hold up a red, blue, or yellow colored block or object and ask children what color it is. Once the color name is given, have children find other objects around the room of the same color. Repeat this with all three primary colors.

Next, tell the children that they are going to hear some grown-up words. When they are ready, have them practice saying *primary* and *secondary*. Tell them that red, blue, and yellow are primary colors. Ask children if they know why.

Explain that red, blue, and yellow are considered *primary* colors because you can mix them and make secondary colors. At this point, hold up a green, orange, or purple block. First, ask children for the name of the color. Then, ask children if they think it is a primary or secondary color. If they answer primary, do not tell them they are wrong. Instead, say, "If red, blue, and yellow are the primary colors, then this must be a s_____ color." (Put in as many syllables needed for them to successfully come up with the answer.) Next, have them find objects with the same color around the room. Repeat this with all three colors.

With each of the secondary colors, point to the primary colors and ask the children to guess what two primary colors make up the secondary color. Encourage their guesses, but lead them to the correct answers.

> red and blue = purple
> red and yellow = orange
> blue and yellow = green

Colors *(cont.)*

HOW *(cont.)*

Children might be curious about different shades of colors. Explain that the shade depends on how much of the primary colors were put in. If more red than yellow is put in, for example, the resulting color will be more reddish-orange.

If a teacher desires, he or she can extend this discussion by asking children if they know other things that are made from basic ingredients. Ask them what they can make using flour and sugar—breads, cakes, and cookies. It depends on how much you add of each thing.

Throughout the year, when asking children what color something is, bring it a step further by asking if it is a primary color or a secondary color. If it is a secondary color, ask what two primary colors make it.

HANDS-ON PRACTICE

Have children trace or color the color names on the Colors Practice pages (pages 297–298). Then, have them color the strips the appropriate colors.

Provide children with red, blue, and yellow paint and three empty cups. Have them make new colors by putting one teaspoon of red and yellow paint in the first cup, red and blue paint in the second cup, and blue and yellow paint in the third cup.

Make copies of the pictures (pages 299–301). Have children paint the pictures the colors directed, using the mixed primary colors to form the secondary colors.

If a teacher wishes to have children experiment with more mixing but does not want to use paint, food coloring works well. One can put a few drops of a primary color in a clear plastic container or cup of water. Add a few drops of a second primary color, and the color change is immediate. One can add more of each primary color and observe how the hue of the secondary color changes. Do this with combinations of blue and yellow, red and blue, and red and yellow.

CLASS EXTENSIONS

Make paper chains using each of these patterns: red, blue, purple; red, yellow, orange; or blue, yellow, green. When making the chains, discuss how red and blue are the primary colors that make up the secondary color purple; red and yellow are the primary colors that make up the secondary color orange; and blue and yellow are the primary colors that make up the secondary color green.

If the materials are available, a teacher can also have his or her students thread colored beads on yarn using these same patterns.

HOME PAGE

Hello,

Today we talked about *colors*. The primary colors are red, blue, and yellow. We discussed how we could mix these primary colors to make secondary colors. Red and yellow make orange. Blue and yellow make green. Red and blue make purple.

This activity helps a child identify colors. It also introduces a child to the idea that different ingredients make different end products.

Entertain your child or help pass the time when waiting by asking questions about color.

Play an "I Spy" game in which your child has to spy what you see. For example, "I see a red car. Can you?" "I see a blue sign. Can you?" "I see a red stripe. Can you?"

Ask your child what colors he or she is wearing. Ask him or her which ones are primary colors and which ones are secondary colors. If a child is wearing a secondary color, ask him or her what two primary colors formed it. Lead your child to the answer by saying, "Hmm, you are wearing a green shirt. Is green made from blue and yellow or red and purple?"

Have fun!

Colors Practice

Cut out the strips and trace the color words. Color the strips to match the color words.

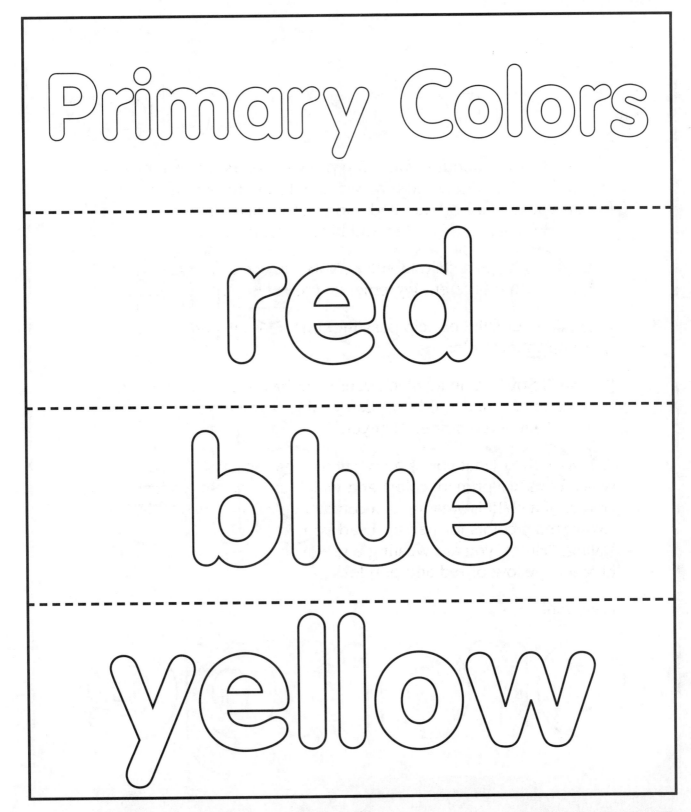

Colors Practice *(cont.)*

Cut out the strips and trace the color words. Color the strips to match the color words.

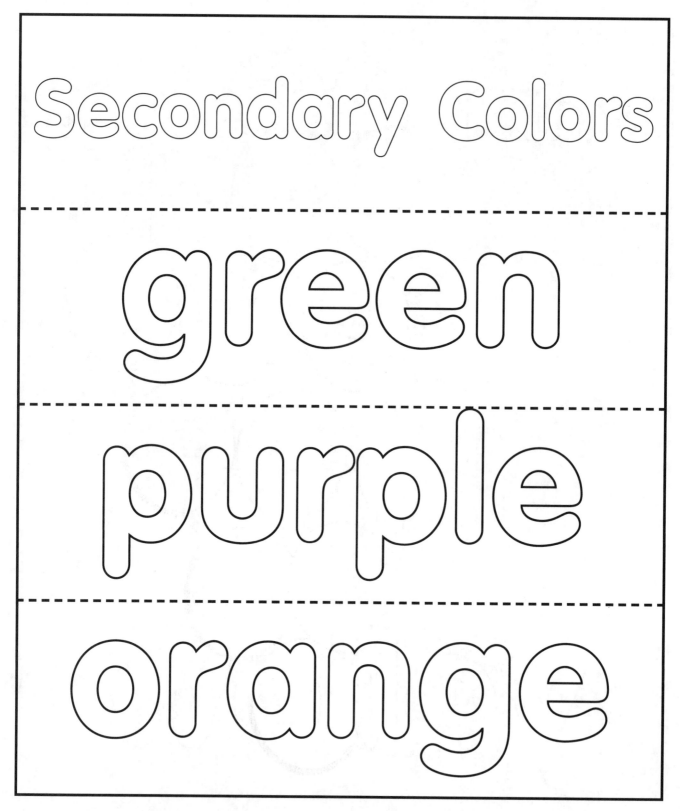

Secondary Colors

green

purple

orange

Name _____

Colors Practice *(cont.)*

Mix blue and red. Paint the picture purple.

Name _____

Colors Practice (cont.)

Mix red and yellow. Paint the picture orange.

Name _____

Colors Practice *(cont.)*

Mix blue and yellow. Paint the picture green.

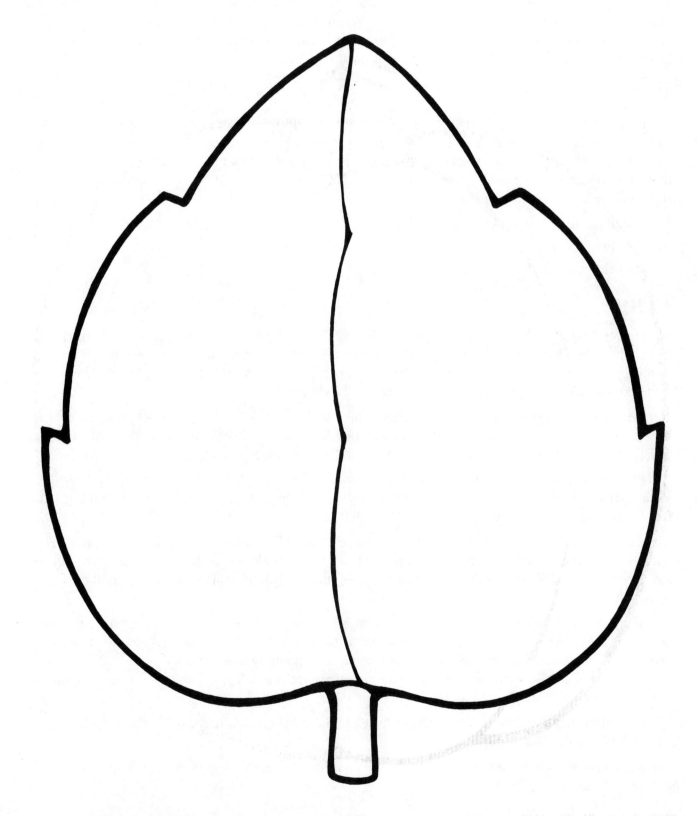

Left and Right

WHAT

We use the words *left* and *right* to differentiate sides or directions. The left sides of our bodies have the left hands. The right sides have the right hands. When we turn left, we turn in the direction of the left sides of our bodies. When we turn right, we turn in the direction of the right sides of our bodies. This lesson deals with left and right, focusing on sides and directions.

WHY

As most children develop, they will favor a particular hand. Some children will show this favoritism earlier than others. Children should never be forced to be right- or left-handed. Whether children will be right-handed, left-handed, or ambidextrous (able to use both the left and the right hand equally well), they need practice distinguishing left from right. Discussion and activities bringing attention to left and right differences can help a child:

- begin to differentiate between left and right
- begin to understand directions and changing points of reference
- develop gross motor coordination

HOW

Start off by having each child raise one arm in the air. Count the number of people who put up left and right hands. Make the comment that everyone tends to have a favorite hand that he or she will do a lot of things with—such as throwing a ball or holding a pencil or toothbrush. Not everyone will have the same favorite hand, but everyone will have a left and right hand.

Next, explain that everyone is going to practice remembering which hand is on the left side and which hand is on the right side. Have the children raise their left hands and shake them. Repeat this with the right hands. Then, have children stamp their left and then right feet.

Engage the children in a game where you call out a side. For example, "Left! Left! Right! Left! Right! Right! Right! Left!" Children respond to your calls by stamping the appropriate right or left foot or shaking or waving the appropriate right or left hand.

You can vary this action by having children sit on their bottoms with their legs on the floor extended out in front of them. As the teacher calls out "Left! Right!," children raise the appropriate foot into the air. If you are outside, you can extend this by having children run or jump to the left or right at every whistle blow.

While children are sitting in a circle, ask them who is to their left. Then have them turn around so they are still in the circle but facing out. Ask them who is to their left now. Repeat this, but this time ask about who is to the right. You can do this same activity by pointing to something in the classroom and asking if it is to a child's left or right. Have them turn around and ask if the object is toward a child's left or right now that they have turned.

If you want greater physical activity, one can have children line up as if they were a train. Call out which direction the "train" needs to turn.

A variation of this would be to lead the "train" in a particular direction and then ask, "What direction did we go? Left or right?"

Left and Right *(cont.)*

HANDS-ON PRACTICE

Sing the song, "The Hokey Pokey." For this song, children stand in a circle and sing:

Put your right hand in,

Take your right hand out.

Put your right hand in,

And you shake it all about.

Do the hokey pokey, (hands up at shoulder sides while you shake them)

And turn yourself about.

That's what it's all about!

(Repeat this verse with left hand, right and left leg, right and left side, and then finally, whole self.)

CLASS EXTENSIONS

Teach this Life Skills Rhyme. It tells which direction to turn if one is unscrewing jar lids, screws, bolts, or faucets.

> Rightie tightie, Leftie loosey.

Have the children repeat it several times and act it out with their hands. Then, have them unscrew several plastic screws or bottles with lids and ask them if the rhyme is true.

You may want to engage the children with silly questions such as these:

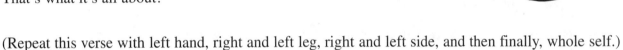

"I have a jar filled with octopus eyes in my hands. Should I go rightie tightie or leftie loosey?"

"Umm . . . hot, hot, hot peppers in this jar. Should I go rightie tightie or leftie loosey?"

"Lots of coins in this money jar. Should I go rightie tightie or leftie loosey?"

"What silly person put all my clothes in this huge jar and screwed the lid down? Should I go rightie tightie or leftie loosey?"

"Oh, no! The water is overflowing from the bathtub onto the floor! What way do I turn the faucet? Should I go rightie tightie or leftie loosey?"

Throughout the year, as children put on their shoes or coats in school, encourage their efforts with the words *left* and *right*. For example, a teacher might say, "Good, you are putting your left shoe on your left foot." "Good, you are putting your right arm in your right sleeve."

A teacher can encourage children to vocalize what they are doing by saying, "I am putting my right shoe on my right foot." "Now, I am putting my left arm into my left sleeve."

HOME PAGE

Hello,

Today we talked about *left* and *right*. We worked on which sides of our bodies left and right refer to. We practiced turning left and right, too. This type of activity can help a child learn to differentiate between left and right. When coupled with movement, it can also help develop physical coordination.

Your child should never be forced to be left-handed or right-handed. It is too early for many children to favor a particular side. No matter what side a child ends up favoring, you can help a child to learn to differentiate between left and right with these activities:

Every time you take a turn in a car, have your child raise the hand that matches which direction you are turning. Then, ask your child, "Are we turning left or right?" As your child begins to develop a better sense of left and right, you can have him or her close his or her eyes when you come to a stop. Have him or her feel if you are turning left or right.

While driving, point out an object and have your child raise or shake the hand that matches which side it is on. Then ask if the object is on the left or right side. For familiar landmarks, bring up how they change "sides" depending which direction you are going. For example, as you go past a school, church, or friend's house, ask which side it is on. Then, when you are driving down the same street in the opposite direction, say, "When we went the other way, the school was on our left. Now which side is it on?"

Note: If a child answers incorrectly, one should not say, "Wrong." Redirect by saying, "It's not on the left, it's on the _____." Once the child responds with the word *right*, say, "Very good! You got it. It's on the right."

You can also reinforce left and right when your child is dressing. For example, you can say, "Now you are putting the left shoe on the left foot." "Now, you are putting your right arm in the right sleeve."

Here is a life skills rhyme for what direction one should turn jar tops, screws, bolts, and faucets:

> Rightie tightie,
> Leftie loosey.

Have fun!